D0880109

OPENING DOORS,
OPENING LIVES

OPENING DOORS, OPENING LIVES

Creating awareness of advocacy, inclusion,
and education for our children with special needs

BY JENNIFER GREENING

FERNE PRESS

Opening Doors, Opening Lives
Creating awareness of advocacy, inclusion,
and education for our children with special needs

Copyright © 2009 by Jennifer Greening
Printed in Canada

Summary: A handbook of how to get children with special needs into the general education classroom.

Library of Congress Cataloging-in-Publication Data
 Greening, Jennifer
 Opening Doors, Opening Lives /Jennifer Greening– First Edition
 ISBN-13: 978-1-933916-42-2
 1. Inclusion. 2. Special-needs children. 3. Autism and related spectrum disorders. 4. Cognitive impairments. 5. General education classroom inclusion. 6. Advocacy for children with special needs.
 I. Greening, Jennifer II. Opening Doors, Opening Lives
 Library of Congress Control Number: 2009929773

This is a true story and several names have been changed.

Any views or opinions presented in this book are solely those of the author and do not necessarily represent those of Nelson Publishing & Marketing/ Ferne Press.

FERNE PRESS

Ferne Press is an imprint of Nelson Publishing & Marketing
366 Welch Road, Northville, MI 48167
www.nelsonpublishingandmarketing.com
(248) 735-0418

Contents

Dedication

To all of our children.
May everyone you meet
recognize your limitless potential.

Acknowledgments

I am appreciative of everyone we meet that looks beyond my child's disabilities and views her as a whole and complete child. I am grateful to the many community organizations our family has relied on for support and advocacy.

There are countless numbers of people in our school community that step outside of their daily roles to look over my daughter. I notice the special recognition my daughter receives from the custodian as we walk by at the end of the day. The secretaries in the office graciously take my calls when my daughter is absent. The people in the cafeteria make sure she has a lunch she enjoys. Administrators and support staff fulfill their roles beyond expectations. And of course, there have been many teachers that have been ready to use their training to make my daughter an important, valued member of her class.

From my daughter, I have found that many lessons can be learned without any words at all. I am grateful for her tolerance of my failures and her willingness to be patient with me. I am very proud of her ability to face the world every day as a child with disabilities. I am continually impressed with her resiliency as she faces a world that is often full of surprises.

I am grateful for my husband, Paul. I appreciate his encouragement and support of "writing a book" being added to our family's daily busy days. He is the anchor of our family and a wonderful, caring father to our children. He created the saying, and tells our children that our last name, Greening, means, "Never, never give up." I am very proud of all our children for their willingness to believe in us.

I am very grateful to my publisher, Marian Nelson, for her ability to see the possibilities with my manuscript. It is an honor to be included in her vision.

I am grateful to my editor, Kris Yankee. I appreciate her encouragement to tell my story, her thoughtful insights, her careful attention to details, and her guidance throughout this process.

I give thanks to God. I humbly feel His guidance as I share His daily message of love and acceptance.

Introduction

I am a mother of three children. My oldest child has special needs. At first glance, you may see that she walks unsteadily. She is unable to speak. She may only briefly make eye contact with you. But if you take a second look, you will see her slight grin, a twinkle in her eyes, and her great desire to make sense of the world around her. I do not see her disabilities. Some people call this denial. I see her endless potential and great possibilities.

Because she is non-verbal, I have changed her name in this book until she finds her voice and gives me permission to use it.

Basically, I have been blessed with a child that, like all children, needs to be educated. Since my child has special needs, educating her is complicated.

I am not writing this book as an expert of inclusive education. There is an entire body of research and experts in this field. Rather, I am writing this book as a parent of a child with special needs. My perspective is different because I am also a public school teacher.

I have come to the conclusion that the best education for all children occurs among their same-age peers in their neighborhood schools. I believe there is too much precious time wasted deciding how to separate our children.

I am fortunate that I have been teaching for eighteen years and hold a few degrees in the field of elementary education. I have learned my greatest lessons from my daughter and the people working with her.

Chances are if you are reading this book, you are seeking information and support for a child with special needs. You are probably beginning to understand that you will not simply be sending this child to school as easily as other children.

Our youngest child is four years old. He attends preschool. I registered him, brought in his paperwork, and he started preschool. His brother is nine years old. He attends our neighborhood elementary school. Again, I registered him, brought in his paperwork, and he started attending our neighborhood school.

Our oldest child is eleven years old. In order for her to attend our neighborhood school, my husband and I have spent hundreds of hours in meetings with school staffs. We sign official documents outlining her educational plans. We must convince the teachers and many members of our community that she belongs at our local school. Every day I work to keep her in school.

I have written this book because I have learned a lot about having a child with special needs. I have met many people in similar situations. I hope this book helps you avoid the pitfalls of educating your child. I hope it helps us move closer to sending all our children to school with a daily feeling of love and acceptance.

Many special educators call the students in their classrooms "their kids." However, I have come to the clear realization that my daughter is clearly *my* child. I have the responsibility of her entire life. In order to provide her with a quality life, I must provide her all the typical memories of childhood. One of the greatest childhood memories is going to school.

If you are reading this book, you are probably looking for some helpful advice. My intention is to give you some guidance based on my experience as a parent and as a teacher in the public schools. It was my intention to tell our story when our journey was "done."

But since there are children starting school every day, I know this cannot wait!

The advocate that supported us once said to me, "Are you sure you want to do this? I wouldn't send anyone I cared about on this road." I think she was saying that it would be easier to allow my child to be sent to a separate school. I would be taking on a great job of sending my child to our neighborhood school. But haven't we all learned that the best decisions are not always the easiest paths to take?

If you want your child with disabilities fully included in public schools, then you must be fully dedicated to this.

> To fully include your child in public school, you must be fully dedicated since it will require daily, unwavering, diligent attention.

It will require your daily, unwavering, diligent attention. People will often say things to you that will make you cry. They will seem to forget they are speaking to this child's parent. You will be busy "clearing the way" for your child's daily successes at school. However, I believe the reward of having my daughter fully included in her local public school has been worth the effort. She is experiencing a typical, joyful childhood. And as her mother, I believe giving her this opportunity is my responsibility.

My husband constantly reminds me, "Jen, save our family first and the world second." I try to remain focused on my job of advocacy for our daughter with special needs. This means that I am her greatest fan. I am the constant, resolute, daily voice of believing that a child with special needs belongs in school—their neighborhood school.

You must understand that if you want your child to be educated in the public school system along with their peers you are taking on an incredibly time-consuming and frustrating job. However, if you have a child with special needs, you have probably already developed some life skills that will help you in your journey. In addition, there is nothing in the world more rewarding than providing your child with the wonderful, typical memories of a childhood filled with laughter and children their own age.

The point of this book is not to convince you that the general education setting is best for your child. You cannot begin the journey of full inclusion in the general education setting for your child with any doubts that you are making the right decision.

This book is written to help you and your family support your child with special needs once you have decided that you want your child educated in the general education setting—your neighborhood school. If you find yourself frustrated and worried, and you experience times of actually crying during a meeting, then you are probably doing things right. If you have moments where you are questioning your skills as a parent, then you are also on the right track.

So, give me your hand and I will guide you through the basics. You will do all the work on your own. Having a child with special needs successfully and fully included in their neighborhood school is bigger than a full-time job.

If you are reading this book:

- You understand that your neighborhood school is the school your child would be assigned to if they did not have special needs.

- You want your child included in their neighborhood school.

- You are willing to revisit the hopes and dreams you had for your child before you learned they had special needs.

Chapter 1
Our Beginning

My husband and I have been married for fourteen years. We live in my hometown in Southeastern Michigan. Our home was carefully selected as the perfect place to raise our family. We have great schools within walking distance of our home.

Shortly after discovering I was expecting our first baby, we put locks on all our cupboards. We spent hours reading baby books. Months before our baby was born, we used the books to select the perfect name for our child. We would call her Marissa. I carefully wrote her name on the Christmas presents we bought and wrapped for her in October.

We charted Marissa's growth month by month in my pregnancy as we looked forward to her arrival. We dreamed about our new life as parents. We looked forward to all of Marissa's firsts—sitting up, crawling, and walking.

Finally, our first child was born. On a cold fall day, we made our way to the hospital using exactly the route we had carefully planned. Our life together was unfolding as we had expected. We fell in love, got married, bought our first home, and now our beautiful child was here. We welcomed her into the world with all the hopes and dreams we have for all of our children. We expected life would unfold according to our careful plans.

After a long delivery, the day arrived to bring our daughter home. According to our plan, I would breastfeed. I charted her feeding times, and we planned our days around her schedule. I noticed I needed to give her head a lot of support, but since she was my first child I did not understand that this was unusual.

As each month passed, we noticed Marissa was not reaching the milestones that we had anticipated.

According to the charts at the doctor's office and the records in our baby books, all babies have a typical rate of development. At the two-month appointment, we reported Marissa was cooing, smiling, and laughing, but she still had trouble holding her head steady. The doctor explained that children with low muscle tone often catch up. He told us not to worry.

At the three-month appointment, the doctor held Marissa and tried to get her to stand. Marissa did not have enough tone in her muscles to bear weight.

At her four-month appointment, she was just starting to hold her head steady. According to the books we were studying, she was supposed to be rolling over.

As each month went by, the doctor gave us hope that she would catch up the following month. We started making her milestone doctor appointments a month later than typically scheduled so she would have some extra time to acquire these skills.

We hoped Marissa would meet each milestone before having to face the doctor at the next well-child doctor appointment. However, at each appointment the pediatrician documented that she was not doing what other children her age were expected to be doing.

By her first birthday, she was beginning to independently sit up but she was not anywhere close to being able to walk. The hope that she would eventually catch up and reach her milestones ended. Marissa still had very low muscle tone. She had just started sitting up. She was not crawling. She did not bear weight through her legs. The doctor began referring us to other doctors, "specialists," to determine why Marissa was not meeting her developmental milestones. Slowly we began to realize life was not unfolding according to our plan. It was during this time we realized our precious first child, Marissa, had special needs. Sadly, we learned our story was not uncommon.

Since Marissa's first birthday, we have taken her to the pediatric neurologist, pediatric ophthalmologist, pediatric orthopedic doctor, and anyone else we heard might help her. Marissa has endured many programs, therapies, and procedures. She wore a hip brace at night to help develop her hip sockets that are usually developed by standing. At home, we placed her in a standing frame twice a day to develop her hips. She had eye surgery to help the eye muscles work together.

Slowly we began to realize life was not unfolding according to our plan.

My husband and I prayed together outside of the MRI and CAT scan rooms as we waited for the answers to why Marissa's development was delayed. According to all her testing, there was nothing medically diagnosed as causing her delays. Her brain appeared normal. Her genetic testing came back normal. Her muscle tone seemed to be improving with time. The doctors explained that it was very common not to know the cause of a child's delay. I thought doctors could always find a diagnosis.

The toddler years of uncertainty and doctor's appointments were exhausting. We had so many questions. Why had she not reached her milestones? What could we do to help Marissa?

Those early years of her life had not been what my husband and I had imagined. We were expecting a child with typical needs. After all, until Marissa was born, we did not know anyone that had a child with disabilities.

While Marissa eventually met the developmental milestones of sitting up and rolling over, her development was considered delayed since she did not meet the milestone at the typical rate of development. Along with her delayed physical milestones, Marissa had not developed any formal language. She made many vocal sounds, but she did not speak.

We felt desperate to get answers that would help our daughter. We researched outside of our typical medical supports and sought the advice of holistic doctors. According to the holistic doctors we visited, it was possible Marissa's delays were brought on by the first vaccination she received in the hospital. It was also possible her delays were caused by environmental factors that we had not discovered. We reacted to this news much like we responded to most of the information we received throughout our journey—with surprise and disbelief. However, regardless of the cause of Marissa's delays, we needed to focus on preparing Marissa for her future.

As our story unfolded, we realized there were many people and many organizations to help us. While the information seemed newly discovered, we realized it was only newly discovered by us. I have included all the resources that I found helpful in the bibliography section at the end of this book.

There are groups of doctors in the DAN (Defeat Autism Now) community that are working to treat children with varied spectrum disorders. There are other organizations dedicated to helping families that have children with special needs. We learned The Autism Society of America had many resources to help us. They helped us ask the right questions at our doctor's appointments and guided us to new therapies.

In addition to the recommendations from the medical community and the therapists, we needed an ongoing program to address Marissa's education. We could not wait until she responded to therapies to address her curiosities and desire to learn. We could not let Marissa's silence overrule her need for rich conversations.

The Arc (formerly known as The Association for Retarded Citizens) also provided many educational opportunities for us. This is a national advocacy organization for people with disabilities. We had many questions: What does the research say about educating a child with special needs? How do we provide a rich childhood for her in our community?

> There are organizations dedicated to helping families that have children with special needs.

We learned that we needed to focus on providing Marissa with a typical childhood. Within the typical childhood lessons, she would learn and develop her skills. Meanwhile, we needed to keep in mind that our end goal was for her to live independently from us.

We have struggled with Marissa's education. On some days our American dream of an education for our daughter turned into a nightmare. As good parents, we believed it was our responsibility to make sure our children were well educated. However, we soon learned that educating Marissa would be complicated.

On many days we felt alone in our struggles to help our daughter. There were many experts giving their opinions, but ultimately, the responsibility of her well-being was with us. Once in a while someone stepped outside of their role and reached out to help us. On those rare occasions we were pointed in the right direction.

Important Points to Remember

- Many developmental delays are not identified at birth.

- It is common *not* to have a specific medical diagnosis for delays.

- Seek out the support of local organizations (see bibliography).

- Ask many questions about the services that support organizations provide.

- Embrace the wisdom and love brought into your life by having a child with disabilities.

Chapter 2
Parent as Advocate

When Marissa was one year old, I received a phone call from my younger brother. While we had always been close, it was very unusual for him to call me. He carefully began our conversation by asking me what the doctors were telling us about Marissa's development. I told my brother not to worry. The pediatrician assured us Marissa's development was a little behind a typically developing one-year-old, but that she would catch up.

My brother frankly said, "Do you know there is physical therapy equipment for babies?" My brother had just started a cleaning business, and he explained he saw small equipment in the physical therapy office for children.

He was concerned about Marissa's development. Many people had asked us, "What do the doctors say?" We all seemed satisfied with the doctor's explanation that she would eventually catch up. It seemed to relieve us from taking ownership of the problem.

This was the first time I considered the possibility of telling the doctor what I wanted for Marissa. I had always thought the doctors were supposed to tell me what to do.

I slowly replied, "No, I didn't know about physical therapy for children."

I could tell he was nervous because he spoke quickly. My brother explained that he believed we were good parents. He hoped I did not feel like he was interfering in our business. He said he loved Marissa too, and he was concerned about her. I told him that it had not occurred to me to ask for further assistance for Marissa. I thanked him for calling and assured him that I would inquire about physical therapy for Marissa.

At Marissa's next doctor's appointment, the doctor quickly noted Marissa's lack of progress. As he began to close her chart, I stopped him. I told him I had spoken with my brother. I learned there was physical therapy for children. I told him I wanted a referral for Marissa to attend physical therapy.

The doctor looked up from Marissa's chart as he considered my request. As he reopened her chart, he slowly explained that indeed there was physical therapy for children. He told me that these referrals usually go through the county agencies. The agencies then contact the local school districts. He told me he would make a referral to the county agency and the local school district would contact us.

I left the doctor's office with a great feeling of accomplishment and guilt. Marissa was going to get help. She was going to get physical therapy. What if my brother had not called me? How much longer would she have gone without help? Until now, I had not considered my role as an advocate for my daughter. In order to ask the right questions, I needed to be educated about the possibilities for Marissa every time I entered an "expert's" office with her.

The next week, a physical therapist and a nurse from our local school district made a home visit to evaluate our daughter. They confirmed what we already knew.

At the following visits to the pediatrician, he seemed more thoughtful in ways

> *I need to be educated about the possibilities for my daughter every time I enter an "expert's" office.*

Marissa could be helped. He began referring us to specialists. Our calendar began to fill up with doctor's appointments and therapy sessions.

During this turbulent time of various doctor's appointments, I was in my seventh year of teaching elementary school. I decided to take a leave of absence. I used this time to be Marissa's coach and advocate. I listened carefully at each appointment, and I asked many questions. I believed there was a program, service, or doctor that would meet her needs. I would spend my days looking for it. I would later realize that my general education training would create the opportunities for her to make progress.

After the doctor's referral to the school physical therapy program, I expected a very strategic, well-planned design for Marissa's support. My concerns were very great and very immediate. I was afraid she would not be ready for school.

The next week, my husband and I met with the physical therapist and the nurse to discuss the results of their testing. We met at an elementary school in our school district. They explained that this is where the baby and preschool programs took place for children with special needs. We were told that since Marissa was behind in her development, she was eligible to receive individual physical therapy sessions twice a week. They also explained that there was a once-a-week parent-child program that I should plan on attending with Marissa.

When we left the meeting, I was relieved we had assistance for Marissa. However, I was so focused on getting help for Marissa that I had not considered we were starting a special education program. I had not considered that there may be an inclusive approach to her assistance. I did not ask if her services could take place in a neighborhood preschool. I was thrilled she was getting help. I happily agreed that I would bring my one-year-old to a special-needs school in our district for the parent-child class and for physical therapy.

My feeling of being thrilled quickly changed. The following

week, I brought Marissa to the parent-child class. There were fifteen children in the "class" ranging from six months to three years. All the children had a range of disabilities. I felt sad seeing the children's struggles. I thought the sessions would eventually get easier for me. However, all the parent-child sessions were hard for me. It was difficult for me to see so many children struggling to roll over or sit up. I was upset that Marissa had difficulties and that she was behind in her development. I felt even worse because we were taken away from a typical, natural childhood environment. I did not know any of the other mothers. We were grouped together because the focus was on our children's disabilities.

At each parent-child class, Marissa and I were surrounded by children with a variety of disabilities, including feeding tubes, Down's syndrome, and other medical diagnoses I did not understand.

In a typical setting, there are a natural proportion of children with disabilities. This means there may be one or two children out of several hundred children that have severe disabilities. The only children in this particular program had disabilities.

I also noticed that no two children experienced their disabilities in the same way. How could such a large and diverse group of children be put together based solely upon the criteria that they had a disability?

There were no typically developing children enrolled at this school. Marissa and I spent time using the mats, toys, and swings to help her build her strength. I was envious of the mothers that had older siblings with them. Their children with special needs had other children to interact with. They had good models of how to use the equipment, and their siblings encouraged them to respond.

I knew from my educational training that children begin forming their self-images very early in life. Would Marissa view herself as only a person with disabilities? Would she feel separate from her peers?

In order to provide some normalcy in our lives, I also enrolled Marissa in a preschool at a local church. There, she had the interest and attention of other children, but she did not have the equipment to support her physical needs.

I later learned that I could have requested special education support in preschool. This would have allowed Marissa to develop typical peer interactions and use her supports at the same time.

Important Points to Remember

- If a doctor has a concern about your child, ask them to discuss the possible treatment options. In order to ask the right questions, you need to be educated about these options prior to arriving at the appointment.

- Public schools offer special education services to children with special needs prior to a child being school age.

- If you have been given a professional recommendation, take the time to ask, "What are other possible ways of addressing this?"

- Seek out peer groups for social interaction for your child.

Chapter 3
Therapy and Advocacy

When Marissa was two years old, we spent our days traveling to many doctor and therapy appointments. I loaded the CD player in my van with the most popular children's music. I was determined to make every minute count toward her education.

I continued to provide Marissa with childhood experiences. I maintained play dates and social gatherings with our neighbors. It was within these experiences that we returned to our familiar surroundings and we received encouragement. In these gatherings, Marissa had the desire to practice what she had been learning in therapy.

When Marissa was three years old, I explained to the physical therapist that I was spending a lot of money on toys that would keep Marissa's attention and meet her developmental needs. She was excited to tell me about a toy lending library at our local Arc organization and handed me a flyer that was sitting on the information table in the hallway.

There was a list of wonderful things the Arc did for people in the community. I quickly skimmed the flyer looking for something about a toy lending library. I saw information about toys. Then I noticed there was a small fee to join the Arc. I called my mom. I expressed my exasperation over trying to save money on toys by spending money to join the Arc. My mom told me she would pay for our membership to the Arc and go with me if I wanted to try it.

Look for local organizations that provide support to families of children with special needs.

I contacted the Arc, and the director explained the toy lending library was called the Lekotek Program (see bibliography). In our county, the Lekotek Program was located in the same building as the Arc. She explained that the director of the Lekotek Program would call me to schedule an appointment.

The next day, the Lekotek leader called. She explained that she liked to have play sessions with the parents and the child so she could offer suggestions on how to play with the child. I was tired from all our other appointments, but I agreed to make the appointment. I appreciated the Lekotek leader's interest in Marissa's progress.

We left our first appointment with several toys that proved to be very helpful. It was nice having a new variety of interesting toys to continue to encourage Marissa's development. She now had toys that would light up at her eye level when she was on her tummy, encouraging her to stay longer in the correct position to develop her stomach muscles. She had toys she could easily interact with while she was positioned in a standing frame at a table developing her hips.

I continued to schedule monthly play sessions at the Arc for Marissa. One day at our monthly play session, the Lekotek leader asked me how things were going for Marissa at school.

I told the Lekotek leader I was frustrated with Marissa's school experience. I explained that since Marissa was now three years old and not yet talking, speech class was added. I explained that I had hoped to have more influence on the selection of her teacher.

I also explained that our meetings did not seem to start on time and paperwork was not complete. I felt a great responsibility to Marissa to get her the best programs, and yet I did not feel like I was being effective.

The Lekotek leader quietly said, "We have someone here that could go with you to meetings. It is part of the service we provide through the membership fee you paid."

Later, I spoke to that person—the Educational Advocacy Director, Maria. She explained that it was her job to go to meetings with parents and to help them with their child's education. She told me that the advocate does not come to meetings with their own agenda. She would be there to help communicate our hopes and dreams for our daughter. Maria told me she wanted to know my wishes for the meeting outcome and that she would attend the meeting with us.

An advocate can help parents with their child's education.

I told Maria that even with my teaching experience, I did not feel like my input was valued in the educational decisions being made for Marissa. They seemed to insist that I trust their experience.

Maria explained that it was important to build a team of people to help Marissa.

"A team of people?" I asked

I told her that I just wanted to know who was in charge of this educational process for Marissa. I wanted to tell this person that I felt like I was not being heard and I needed more educational research presented to me with their decisions. As Marissa's mother, I wanted to feel like my opinions seemed very important to them.

Maria quietly explained that she understood my frustrations. She also patiently explained that no one person is in charge.

It is important to build a team of people to help your child.

I screeched, "No one is in charge of this?"

She flatly replied, "Nope. Not really. It is important to build a team of people to help Marissa. The principal is as close as you are going to get to someone in charge, but she is actually considered an equal member of the team."

Maria patiently explained that there is an Individualized Educational Plan (IEP) process that has been created to support children with special needs. All of the plans for Marissa's education would take place within the IEP process. This means that anyone involved in Marissa's education would meet to decide her educational goals and services. My heart sank. I felt like I was going in circles. I felt frustrated.

IEP meetings were routinely part of my role as a teacher. I attended the meeting, gave my input, and went on to the next scheduled event of my day. I had never considered the consequences of my opinions in the IEP meetings. Once in a while a parent cried, but I just attributed it to the parent feeling overwhelmed. As the teacher, I did not feel much of an obligation to make this process any easier for the parent. I was just doing my job. Now, as a parent, I saw the IEP much differently.

As agreed, Maria attended our next IEP meeting at the school where Marissa was getting physical therapy. The only thing she asked me to do was to let the principal know I would be bringing an advocate with me. She explained it was important to ease any worries and to explain the advocate was coming to help us at the meeting. So I did as she requested. I called the principal of the school. I was friendly. I explained that the advocate asked me to call. To my surprise, she told me that many people bring advocates with them to meetings.

My husband and I had also been in touch with a special education attorney. The attorney said she was not needed unless we felt there was an irresolvable problem. However, the attorney told me we could hire her to attend the meetings too. I was so busy understanding my advocate's role and the IEP process that I had not discussed the attorney with my advocate.

I then said to the principal, "We called a special education attorney, and we called an advocate. Do you think we need them both at our meetings?"

Looking back, this conversation seems funny to me. I was so busy being a good mother to Marissa that I had not considered her reaction. She quickly replied, "Oh no. That is not needed. Usually bringing an advocate is enough. Involving attorneys makes it much more complicated."

This was great advice. Had I thought to ask, our advocate probably would have said the same thing. We wanted to be involved in Marissa's educational decisions. We did not want attorneys to determine what was best for her. However, it was probably okay for the principal to know that we had spoken to an attorney and that we were prepared to do anything to provide our daughter with the very best education. As a new parent to this IEP process, I was truly asking for her opinion. I think if I had purposely threatened to bring an attorney, I would have created a climate of distrust.

It was finally time for our first IEP meeting with our advocate by our side. Now it was my turn again to sign on the line that said "parent." I watched as all the experts signed on the lines previously reserved for me as a teacher.

I had attended IEP meetings for Marissa when we added the speech class. Our meeting did not start on time. Paperwork was filled in as we sat and waited. We did not seem to agree about what we had discussed at the previous meeting. I felt like it was just our word against their word.

Sitting at this IEP felt like we were watching a movie for a second time. We were in the same room. All the same people attended the meeting. We were looking at the same IEP document. The only difference was that our advocate was sitting next to us.

As the meeting started, I noticed there was a much more professional tone to the meeting. Our meeting started on time. All the paperwork was done and actually typed. Everyone seemed ready to address our concerns.

With our advocate by our side, we felt like we had someone helping us.

One of the teachers began, "It is possible we can have Marissa see a combination of the two speech teachers you are requesting. We do not normally do this, but we think we have figured out a way this will work." Our advocate had not said a word. How could this be? Just last week, my request to have input for my daughter's class seemed impossible. Now this week it can happen? Just the presence of an advocate at the meeting changed the entire meeting. In addition, our advocate was taking notes. We felt like we had someone helping us.

Marissa would remain in this educational setting until it was time for her next evaluation. Our advocate cautioned us about allowing unnecessary evaluations of Marissa. She explained that evaluations could be used as "evidence" to change Marissa's educational placement.

Important Points to Remember

- Take time to have conversations with the people interacting with your child. Their informal opinions and advice are usually very helpful.

- Discover the full range of support and services that organizations in your community provide.

- Search your local organizations for an advocate to join you at meetings.

- Prior to attending a meeting with an advocate, inform the principal that an advocate will be joining the meeting to help you.

- Bring a picture of your child with you. It may help you remain focused on the needs of your child.

- Attend meetings in the true spirit of working together in the best interest of your child.

- Always be polite, kind, and professional.

- Arrive at meetings a few minutes early. The most important conversations seem to take place outside of the official meeting time.

Chapter 4
Evaluations

After three years of physical therapy, occupational therapy, speech therapy, and parent-child classes, we agreed to another evaluation of Marissa, to be conducted by the school personnel. Our advocate, Maria, explained that the purpose of the evaluation needed to be very clear.

We had been able to put off the "standard/required" evaluations for years. Maria explained that if we were happy with Marissa's placement, there was no need for an evaluation.

However, the evaluations began. Marissa was four years old. We requested to have her tested for autism. We were told the teachers from the school for children with autism would come to evaluate Marissa.

"There is a completely separate school for students with autism?" I meekly asked. How could I be a teacher and not know about this other school for children in my community?

I wanted Marissa to have typical childhood experiences. I did not want her separated from her peers. However, we felt assured the evaluations would be very helpful in assessing Marissa's needs.

I trusted that everyone understood my wishes for Marissa. I anticipated a recommendation that would come close to honoring my desire for Marissa to be included with her neighborhood peers. The evaluations took place over several weeks. The teachers from the school for children with autism came to the elementary school where Marissa was being evaluated. I met them. They looked at Marissa for a couple of minutes while she sat next to me in a stroller. They quickly said to me, "It is obvious Marissa is too smiley and interactive to be autistic."

The evaluations continued periodically for the next two weeks. The physical therapist and the speech teacher took turns conducting most of the evaluations. They asked Marissa to stack blocks and give them shapes. They noted her physical difficulty of not being able to walk and her inability to talk. I wondered how Marissa was supposed to stack blocks to "prove" her intelligence when she had low muscle tone and she could barely lift her arms.

A month later, the results of the evaluations were formally written. I told my husband that I was sure they were going to recommend the PPI program—a separate preschool program that took place in the elementary school. It was a preschool only for children with special needs. I was not happy about Marissa being placed in a separate school setting, but I thought it would only be temporary, until she started school. I thought we could try it.

I typed my requests of what I needed for her in that classroom. Once she made this transition, I wanted to make sure she had the same physical therapist and speech therapists. I put Marissa in the car and brought her to the school with me for her physical therapy appointment and to get the testing results.

Marissa lay on the floor next to me while I received the results. I learned that since Marissa had more than one disability—she could not walk or talk—she would be considered "cognitively multiply impaired." I further learned there were special schools in the neighboring cities for children with this label. I was told that my husband and I were expected to give input on which one of the separate schools we would send her to.

I thought of the typed list in my pocket for the PPI program. It was not recommended to place Marissa in the separate classroom— it was recommended that Marissa be placed in a separate school.

I was told that if I truly wanted the best for my daughter, I would send her to a school for children with disabilities. I was told that the separate schools would have the best physical therapists, speech therapists, and programs to meet the unique needs of my daughter.

Inclusion in a general education school was not mentioned. I felt foolish for trusting anyone else to do what I believed was Marissa's best interest. Some parents think the school for children with special needs is okay, but for my daughter I really wanted her in her neighborhood school.

I held back my tears. I took the directions to the schools and assured them we would make appointments to visit. I smiled at Marissa, "Okay, honey, let's go." I helped her hold onto her small child-size walker. I helped her guide the walker down the hallway and into the parking lot.

I immediately called my husband. As the tears rolled down my face, I pulled out the typed list for the PPI class. I blurted out, "Paul, they didn't recommend for Marissa to attend the PPI program. They recommended a completely separate school!"

In a calm, gentle voice he said, "Jen, we will work this out. Let's go look at the schools and then we can decide."

We made appointments to visit the schools the next week. We agreed to take Marissa with us so they could meet her.

As we walked into each school, we noticed immediately they did not sound like the schools we knew. As we visited each classroom, we noticed we did not hear any children talking or laughing. We realized that many of the children in the classrooms we visited could not speak. The only sound of talking came from the adults.

There were mats and metal equipment. We did not see a library. Marissa tried to leave the rooms and would not stay with us. Paul agreed to take Marissa to the gym so I could talk with the teachers.

I don't know why we agreed to take Marissa with us. I don't know why I expected her not to be afraid or worried. She enjoyed being in environments with children she knew and with children that talked to her. I could not think of any typically developing children that would be expected to make such a dramatic change. Over time, I learned that children with special needs are asked to do many things we would never ask of typically developing children.

Against my better judgment, and in contrast to my teacher training and experience, my husband and I agreed to send our daughter to the school for children with special needs in the next city.

Important Points to Remember

- It is important that you understand the purpose of a formal evaluation being conducted at school.

- It is extremely difficult for a non-verbal child to prove their intelligence.

- It is my understanding that parents must sign a form to grant permission for formal testing such as IQ testing.

- The IEP team determines the best educational placement for the child—not the test results.

- Very often, parents are the key to deciding where their child is educated.

- Children with special needs are often expected to make transitions and adjust to circumstances that we would not expect from general education students.

Chapter 5
Separated

Our first experience at the school for children with special needs began with a meeting. We sat in the office at an oval table big enough for all the staff members that would be working with Marissa. Our advocate joined this meeting too.

We were told that Marissa would be expected to ride the school bus to and from school. They explained it was good for her to begin learning independence. The other six people from the school sitting at the table with us seemed to nod in agreement.

I looked at everyone and thought about the young children that lived in my neighborhood. There was not one child being asked to go anywhere without their mother. Marissa had just turned five years old. I was expected to put my baby on a school bus every morning? I felt desperate.

I found my courage and said, "No, I will drive Marissa to school every day. I think this is best for her."

It seemed like they were ready for my reply. They explained they would honor "the mother's" decision for now. I never knew the word "mother" could hurt my feelings. It seemed so impersonal. My child was coming to a different city, and they didn't seem to even know my name.

They explained they would create a plan to gradually transition Marissa into riding the bus to school. Compromise. No longer could I be the only voice in what I thought was best for my daughter. We had entered the IEP process—everyone had an opinion on what happened at school for my daughter.

I started driving Marissa to school every day. School buses lined the back of the building from fourteen school districts in the county.

> Once the IEP process began, we realized that everyone had an opinion on what would happen at school.

Marissa attended school in one of the oldest buildings in the neighboring city; it was built in the early 1900s. It was three stories, with a tiny elevator for everyone to share, and a big staircase if your child could manage it. There were approximately one hundred fifty students. I did not see any student in the school walking into the building.

Paraprofessionals waited outside to greet the students in their wheelchairs and to take the children to the elevator. They took turns waiting for the elevator. The students were then wheeled from the elevator to the hallway outside their classrooms.

Although there were other students in wheelchairs, I wanted Marissa to walk into the building. First of all, the orthopedic surgeon and physical therapists were telling us to have her walk longer distances. Secondly, I did not feel it was in Marissa's best interest to consider herself as confined to a wheelchair when we were trying to build a desire for her to walk.

As a teacher, I learned that schools should be designed around students' needs. However, many decisions in schools seem to continue to be made for the adults and for the structure of the schools. Sometimes I feel like it is difficult to have personnel put aside their needs and the structure of the school and look at my child's needs.

As Marissa's mother, I could not bring myself to put her in a wheelchair because there was an old elevator in an old building. I saw the problem as many children waiting for an elevator, rather than Marissa needing a wheelchair.

Why were there daily long waits for an elevator at a school supposedly designed to meet the needs of children with special needs? Essentially, I felt like they were asking me to consider the problem of an inefficient system of getting all the children on the elevator. My focus was only on what was best for my daughter.

After getting up to their classrooms, the children would sit in the hallways in their wheelchairs and wait. All the children in their wheelchairs were lined up next to each other. I was told the students would wait in the hallway until the teachers arrived in the classrooms and it was time for school to begin.

Again, while they waited, since most of the children were non-verbal—there was no sound of children talking. I looked at their faces and I wondered why their parents had decided to send them here. I supposed they had been told what I had been told—their neighborhood school could not meet "their needs." I learned that some parents had actually been told their child would not be safe in an elementary school.

The next time I called our advocate, I asked her, "How could our local neighborhood school, a school created to educate 'the public,' not be designed to meet the public's needs?"

Maria had a daughter with disabilities. It seemed she had already considered my question years before I asked. Maria explained that she believes that schools should be designed to meet the needs of all children. And that people in the community—in public—are going to have disabilities. It is a natural occurrence of being human.

Some parents that I had met believed the public school was not safe for their child with disabilities. They were worried that they would be teased by others. The parents also worried that their children would not be supervised on the playground.

In all my years of teaching, I had never considered that people would not feel safe at school. I was always told that schools must be safe for all children.

As a teacher, I didn't allow children to exclude others. I do not think we should permit our public schools to be designed to exclude anyone. I believe children need to learn among their peers.

Then I thought, "What am I doing?" Poor Marissa was experiencing the most extreme form of separation only because she had disabilities. Who had decided that one needed to prove one's "intelligence" to attend public schools?

After our next IEP meeting, I asked Maria, "Why are these children going to this separate school?"

Maria replied, "The parents determine where their children go to school. There isn't anyone in this building that couldn't go to a regular school."

I had also been considering this notion, so I challenged her, "What about a child with stomach issues—the child that throws up all the time?"

She replied, "That child will need to learn to carry a bag with them."

Marissa had been seated next to a child that threw up. Since Marissa could not get up and walk, he threw up on her. I also thought it would be better to have him in a school where the children could walk and get up to move if it looked like he was going to get sick.

I noticed that EMS was called at this school often for different medical issues. I did

Special education is a service, not a place.

not think my daughter's education should be disrupted by EMS more often than a general education student. EMS can be called for any school. Any staff member can be well-trained for a child with greater medical needs. If the child needs to be assigned a nurse, then the nurse could be with the child in a general education school.

Our advocate reminded me, "Special education is a service, not a place. Goals and objectives are created in an IEP. Then the parents decide where these goals and objectives are met. Of course, I should be saying the 'team' decides—but I have not met any staff members that insist on placing a child with very special needs in a general education classroom."

Important Points to Remember

- Most general education children do not need to prove their intelligence prior to attending their neighborhood school.

- Parents determine where their children attend school.

- Decide what is most important to you, and tell your advocate about the things you will not compromise.

- Listen carefully before responding in meetings. It is the only way you will appear reasonable.

- You will have to compromise in the spirit of cooperation in the IEP.

- If you disagree, you should be ready to back up your opinion with a reasonable explanation, current educational research, and/or a medical reason.

- Children learn how to be in a general education school by being in a general education school.

Chapter 6
Curriculum

What about the curriculum? How can a general education teacher at our neighborhood school address the needs of so many children? A good teacher does this every year. There is no such thing as an entire class being "at grade level." When I taught fourth grade, I had a range of reading abilities. Some children could not read at all. Some children were reading at a high school level. A good teacher is organized and naturally addresses the learning needs of each individual student in the classroom.

Trying to incorporate the learning needs of a child with disabilities requires that all the best teaching practices are implemented. This means more hands-on, cooperative work that requires more movement. This is just good teaching. When there are no students with special needs in the room, it is easier to move away from these practices. However, when you are educating a child with special needs, good teaching must occur to keep learning happening. This is one reason the test scores of *all* students improve when inclusion happens in schools.

"The research and evaluation data on inclusion indicate a strong trend toward improved student outcomes (academically, behaviorally, and socially) for both special education and general education students" (Libsky, Gartner, 1995).

But what happens when the school insists on a particular program for your child? School staff often say, "Put the child in the cognitively impaired room and 'get them ready' for general education." I believe that this thinking is backwards. My understanding of public school education law is that the child should be *first* placed in the *least restrictive* environment. Learning happens within the environment. A child will naturally have to "get ready" when placed in the general education environment.

~~~~~~~~~~~~~~~~

The child should first be placed in the least restrictive environment.

~~~~~~~~~~~~~~~~

However, I did not have enough experience with inclusion to keep Marissa out of a separate school.

Rather than starting her preschool experience in our neighborhood school, Marissa attended the school for children with special needs. I was not prepared for Marissa's arrival home. When she got off the bus, she looked tired, sad, and pale.

In her classroom, there was one adult for every three children in the room. The only sound of talking in the room was from the adults since none of the children could speak. There was no artwork hanging in the classroom. The few art projects that were completed by the children were sent home.

Since the children were transported from many neighboring cities, we did not know any of Marissa's classmates. Marissa could not talk, so she could not tell us their names. I did not know the paraprofessionals that were taking her to the bathroom. She was being put on the toilet once an hour with a seat belt and told to "go potty."

At the "work table," Marissa was strapped into a brown chair to do her "work." One lesson I observed was a turn-taking lesson. A fuzzy, dancing animal was placed in front of one child at a time.

When it was in front of the child, then the child could push it and make it dance. The other children were also seat-belted into their chairs around the table. They were expected to watch the other children play with this toy. I was told they were "learning to take turns."

This was completely adult directed. Since all the children had limited mobility, there was no natural turn taking among the children. It occurred to me that the staff was doing the best they could to re-create what turn taking was supposed to look like. However, this environment looked nothing like the general education public school.

The talking and laughter that was common at our neighborhood school was absent. In order to develop her language skills, I needed my non-verbal daughter to be surrounded by talking and, more importantly, I needed her to have a great desire to talk to someone. Who was she going to have a conversation with here? Just because she was non-verbal didn't mean that she couldn't hear and understand those around her.

I did not see a library in the school. There were many wheelchairs, chairs with seat belts, mats, and adaptive equipment.

I assumed that they would have a wonderful adaptive playground. However, there was an old wooden structure with a few swings. Our local parks offered a greater variety of maneuverable equipment.

As a general education teacher, I understood that every word I said to the children had the potential of being repeated at home. With Marissa being non-verbal, I worried: How would I know if things were not going well at school? Who would tell me? How would I know Marissa was safe? She could not tell me if someone mistreated her. There were no other children around her that could tell someone if they saw her being mistreated.

I believe that I must have Marissa among very talkative children. I feel they are the best chance I have at helping her stay safe. I think if someone speaks harshly or mistreats her, then chances are this will be repeated at home during someone's dinnertime.

One day, I got Marissa off the bus. Again she looked pale, sad, and tired coming home from school. The bus driver said, "What's up with her shoes?" I looked and saw there was duct tape all around her shoes and around her ankles.

I replied, "I don't know."

I carried my sad daughter into the house. It took me about five minutes to tear off the tape and remove her shoes. I called the school and requested to speak to her teacher. I was sure she would be quite alarmed by what I had to report. I exclaimed, "I just got Marissa off the bus. Her shoes were taped on her feet with duct tape."

The teacher replied, "Yes, she kept using the ledge of the chair to take off her shoes, so we have been taping them on." Instantly I remembered the small pieces of tape I had found on her socks the past few days. I felt terrible that I had been naive and trusting.

I told her firmly, "Do not tape her shoes to her feet. I expect you have better training than that. Think of another way to get her to wear her shoes."

You must pick your battles carefully.

Later, I learned that taping her shoes to her feet was illegal. Yet, you must pick your battles carefully, and my battle was not going to be the tape on her shoes. My battle was going to get my daughter in a general education school.

What concerned me the most was that I felt in this school this seemed to be considered normal. I wanted my daughter in a school where this looked completely ridiculous. I wanted her to learn to behave in a typical way. The only way to do this was to put her in an environment where people behaved in typical ways.

In the spring, it was finally time for the "transition IEP." This meant that staff from our local school district would come to observe my daughter at this school. The day of this meeting was one of the happiest days of my life. Marissa was going to kindergarten at our neighborhood school!

We agreed to borrow the chair with the seat belt for the kindergarten room. Seeing the brown, thirty-year-old chair in the bright, colorful kindergarten room spoke volumes. We appreciated that one of the teachers tried making a cover for it so it would match the beautiful surroundings Marissa was now in.

I was thrilled that Marissa was among children that talked and, more importantly, talked to her! She had models of daily conversations. She had models of running and playing.

Children with special needs require a highly skilled, organized, creative teacher that enjoys learning with others. It is important that your child's teacher's day is preplanned enough to know what your child will be doing throughout the day. It is important to have materials ready in order to tell the paraprofessional what to do.

As a teacher, every year I had students that received support from the special education teacher. As a parent, every year we carefully wrote goals to meet Marissa's individual needs. In order for Marissa to have meaningful lessons, I knew her individual goals needed to be tied to the general education curriculum.

However, I never considered that a special education curriculum did *not* exist. According to START (Statewide Autism Resources and Training), the goals of special education are "accelerated growth toward, and mastery of, state-approved grade-level standards."

Marissa does not come to class with a separate curriculum. She comes with IEP goals. In her case, these twelve goals are the only things she gets evaluated on. She needs to show progress on these twelve goals. Goals in the IEP stay the same for the entire year. The best way for her to reach her goals is to work on them within the context of the daily lessons.

Now that I have a daughter with special needs, I am more sensitive to hearing, "I just deliver the curriculum." This is untrue. Teachers do not simply present material, but must also make sure the children are learning it. They must use their years of training and supplies to figure out how to instruct my daughter. She will not be the only child in the room not performing at "grade level." The ideas teachers create for her will also benefit other children in the class. In addition, they are not alone. Teachers get many people to give them insight on how to do this.

The children with special needs come with all the *services and supports* described in their IEP. Marissa has physical therapy, speech therapy, occupational therapy, adaptive physical education, and access to an inclusion consultant, social worker, behaviorist, augmentative communication consultant, and the school nurse. All of these staff members are involved in planning what she does every day. A good teacher will put these people to work to help them get ideas for lessons for all students.

Marissa has paraprofessional support. Often while the paraprofessional is "assigned" to the child, this person is often helping other students in the classroom. This means there is at least another adult in the classroom every day. When the child is absent, the paraprofessional still comes to work. There are days when the paraprofessional is only working with the general education students.

> Children with special needs come to class with all the services described in their IEP.

If you want your child included in public school, money should never be discussed. It seems like the elephant in the room at each meeting I attend—but no one can deny service because it "costs too much." The burden to make public schools work better for all students is with public schools. I do not have the time or energy to change their structures. I am working around the clock raising a child with special needs.

In an ideal setting, I would like my school and my community to rally around me and support me. It seems like they take the parents with the greatest worries and make them fight for their child's education. The parents are dealing with many serious medical issues. This may be one of the reasons separation of children in public schools continues.

The other reason children remain separate is that unless you, the parent, are a trained public school teacher, how would you know there are such varying educational levels in every grade? If you are not trained in the field, it is best to get help from your advocate and learn as much as you can.

Public school teachers naturally address the learning needs of a variety of students. But something happens when you say the child has "special needs." Many teachers think they are not "qualified" to address the child's needs. General education teachers often have not considered that they may already have training to help. They think as I did when Marissa was young—there must be someone more qualified than I am to help this child.

I traveled around with Marissa seeking experts to address her needs. However, her disability is only one small part of who she is. She needs a teacher skilled at creating social interactions. She needs a teacher who understands where Marissa's learning fits in alongside her peers' lessons.

The special education support staff can help with creating lessons, but I have found that once the teacher understands how to make simple modifications to lessons, then the teacher takes over. For example, in first grade the students were working on writing their letters. Marissa used puffy paint to write letters (with paraprofessional assistance) and an alphabet book to glue pictures of the various letters the class was working on that day. This daily routine stayed the same for the class and for Marissa. A simple modification allowed Marissa to participate in the class writing activity for several days.

The most magical lessons happened when the teacher figured out modifications that worked for Marissa, but also worked for the entire class. One day I saw a teacher turn out the lights and use a flashlight to have the students look at each letter of the alphabet. She kept Marissa's attention. The best thing was that all the students were more attentive and interested in the lesson. Everyone benefited.

When Marissa started kindergarten, she could not walk. She could not come to a standing position without assistance. Physical therapists encouraged me to put desir-

> The typical kindergarten classroom was where Marissa would learn.

able toys on the table and entice Marissa to reach for them. One day, as the daily volunteer, I went to the library with the class. I sat on the floor with the children and listened to the story. When the librarian was finished reading the story, she quietly said, "Now stand up and get your books." With that direction, all the children stood up. And right in front of me, for the very first time, Marissa stood up on her own! Tears instantly fell down my face. I exclaimed, "Marissa is standing! She got up on her own—she has never done this before!" The kindergarten children stopped in their tracks, they turned to look at Marissa, and then they started to clap. It was the support she needed—from her peers. This was the environment she would learn in. This was a natural place to try to stand up in. The other children naturally reinforced her efforts.

In kindergarten, first, second, and third grades, we invited the entire class to her birthday parties. Every year, every child in the class came.

Important Points to Remember

- Request that your child receives a highly skilled, organized, creative teacher that enjoys learning with others.

- There is no such thing as an entire class being "at grade level."

- Studies show test scores of *all* students improve when inclusion is done well in school.

- Services cannot be denied because they "cost too much."

- Keeping a non-verbal child around very talkative children increases your chances of knowing if your child is being mistreated.

- Many people feel as I did when Marissa was young—there must be someone more qualified than I am to help this child.

Chapter 7
Best Practices

Before Marissa started kindergarten, our days were busy with appointments and play dates. In the evenings, I went back to school. I earned another degree in education. This time, I quizzed my professors on the best practices for the leaders, the principals, of schools. I used this time to research special education law and to reaffirm my knowledge about the best educational practices. I suppose I was hoping for an easy solution to my dilemma of educating my daughter. I think every research paper I completed was tied somehow to educating a child with special needs.

At the end of my program, the neighboring school district came to recruit us as principals for their schools. I could not figure out how to be a full-time principal and a mother of two small children. Instead, I decided to return to teaching part time.

I returned with the enthusiasm to make a difference in the lives of my second grade students. My experience as Marissa's mom allowed me to see my teaching profession in a new light. I was excited to have the opportunity to include all children in my instruction in the same school district where I lived. It was my background in education that gave me the knowledge to help all children learn. It was my experience as Marissa's mother that gave me the humility to reach out to all children and to include all children in every learning experience. Realizing there was no magical way to educate a child with disabilities, I felt empowered to use my general education skills to teach all children.

I have always valued everyone working together. I enthusiastically entered my new second grade classroom. But where was *everyone*? Where were the children that looked like my daughter? I was disappointed that I did not have any children with special needs in my general education classroom.

> Being Marissa's mother gave me the humility to reach out to all children and to include all children in every learning experience.

By the second grade, I learned that most of the children that looked like my daughter were in special needs classrooms or in separate schools. In some schools, these children may be in separate classes and then come as visitors to general education classrooms.

I began to realize there was a discrepancy between the education I received and the current practices in many schools.

You have probably wondered: What does the current research say about the best teaching practices? Where should children with special needs be educated? Where should all children be educated? If you want your child included in the general education school, then you need to be educated. It is now common practice to go online to research a medical diagnosis you receive. This helps you make the best decisions about your health. You should also be researching educational recommendations for your child based on the research for the teaching profession.

All general education teachers learn and commonly agree in basic teaching practices. The educational literature refers to these as the "best practices" of teaching.

Teachers agree that it is not best practice to ability-group students. This means they do not keep children at low, medium, and high groups throughout the day. Research shows this hurts children's self-image. Teachers agree that the past practices of creating the good reading group, the Bluebirds, and the poor reading group, the Crows, does not improve reading skills and is not best practice. No matter what names we give to the groups, sorting children like this is harmful.

In addition, teachers are very careful about forming preconceived ideas from past teachers about students. Teachers want to allow the child growth. They do not want to begin "tracking" students. This means that the same low label would follow the students from year to year.

Teachers understand that they teach children to think. They carefully construct questions with Bloom's Taxonomy, which is a method of asking questions to help students develop thinking skills. A few simple questions are okay to ask in order to assess general understanding. Then the teacher moves to higher-level questioning such as, "What do you think will happen next?" Teachers understand that a student that has difficulty with writing may be able to orally answer the higher-level questions. Teachers naturally adjust their teaching to accommodate the needs of a variety of students in their classes. It is possible that the accommodations your child requires may benefit another student in their class.

Teachers respect student confidentiality. This means they do not discuss the needs of the student outside of the professional setting. If your child receives speech services, then your child's teacher will not tell another parent this information.

These practices govern common teaching practices of our profession. What happens when a child is labeled with special needs? Unfortunately, the children with special needs are often put together in separate classrooms or even special schools where everyone knows about their disabilities. Having a child with special needs does not mean that your child needs a separate education. Teachers have already been educated about the harmful effects of separating children.

> Having a child with special needs does not mean that your child needs a separate education.

If you have a child with special needs, your child needs an outstanding education. Your child needs a wonderful teacher that is curious about them. I believe your child needs a teacher ready to incorporate their special education services into a typical, general education classroom.

General education teachers have been trained to address many of your child's needs. Your child will not be the first student that does not read in their class. Your child will not be the first child that has had behavioral difficulty. However, this may be the first time that your child's teacher has been given the trust and the expectation to use their general education training to address your child's needs.

We know children make progress when they are immersed in the best teaching practices. According to teacher training and brain-research practices, all children need quality teaching/learning opportunities.

In my teaching experience, I learned that if my students were not well-behaved, I needed to improve my classroom management skills. In my teacher training, I learned to use many modalities to deliver a lesson. I learned that children need to sit for short periods of time. Most of the

> When a child does not respond to my lesson, I make modifications based on the needs of the child and then try again.

time, children should be involved in hands-on, cooperative group activities.

If the children do not respond to my initial lesson, I need to have a "safety valve" lesson. This is my backup lesson to use if the first lesson seems ineffective. It is not professional to simply report that a child is not responding to my instruction. If the child does not respond to my lesson, then I need to make modifications based on the needs of the child and then try again, and again, and possibly again.

Teachers understand the "Zone of Proximal Development." This means that when a teacher figures out what a child knows and can do, they create lessons to move the child just a little further. When general education teachers learn that Marissa does not speak, some of them automatically feel overwhelmed. They think we will expect the teacher to teach Marissa to talk. This is too big of a leap.

Teachers will learn from her speech teacher that Marissa is using a voice-output device to foster her communication within the classroom. Of course some day we would like her to talk, but according to current educational research, supporting communication will eventually lead to speech.

I was trained to work with parents and to support my instruction with community resources. Teachers have learned the importance of bringing in people from the community for learning opportunities from outside the classroom. Fortunately, if used well, the additional resources brought in with Marissa's support services offer a greater knowledge base and support for her entire class.

Teachers are trained to help children show respect to one another. They address the "Core Democratic Values," which honors the needs of all children in the community and creates wonderful opportunities for children to learn from others.

Teachers know the importance of having a print-rich environment filled with rich conversations. Marissa needs to learn to communicate. A rich environment filled with conversations will help her to develop communication skills.

You have probably been told that your child is "not ready" for a typical learning environment. However, only being in the general education classroom will give your child authentic opportunities to learn how to be in this environment in the first place.

Classrooms are naturally multi-leveled, multi-skilled environments. In your well-thought-out placement, your child will have identified needs and additional staff supports. If you need more information about the supports your child may receive in the classroom, there are many articles written about inclusion. The laws refer to this practice as mainstreaming.

In the past, children had to prove their competence to be allowed into a general education classroom. If your child is nonverbal, then you must presume competence. This is referred to in the research as the "Least Dangerous Assumption". I must presume competence and the ability for the child to understand—only then will I seek creative ways to instruct in reading, social skills, and classroom content.

If an expert has told you that your child does not have any learning potential, then take your child to see a different expert. We know from brain research that the brain continually strives to learn and regenerate itself. We know that a positive self-image and a belief in one's ability directly affect learning. So why would we accept a loss of hope?

If an expert has told you that your child does not have any learning potential, then take your child to see a different expert.

Parents look to schools for guidance in the early preschool years. Sadly, many parents' hopes for their child's education become extinguished. They are told that the general education classroom will not help their child. They are told it is too noisy, too crowded, and unsafe. If this is true, then schools must be restructured for all students. This is one of the myriad of reasons why including children with special needs in schools improves the education of all students. Mediocre educational practices are reexamined to make schools accessible for all learners.

Teachers learn that meeting students' basic needs (food, water, shelter, clothing, sense of security, etc.) and creating a feeling of belonging must occur before any higher educational skills can be mastered. This is known as Maslow's Hierarchy of Needs. When done well, we have learned that inclusion creates an accepting, loving environment ready for higher learning.

Including your child in public schools is a journey. Do your homework. Research recommendations. Are decisions being recommended for your child based upon the best, researched teaching practices or are they made based upon a few people's opinions? It is not responsible or ethical for educators to make recommendations that are not based on sound, researched educational practices. It's a parent's right and responsibility to be up on the latest educational research.

> Do your homework. Research recommendations.

You are not entering the world of education for the experience of one group of people. You are relying on the teaching profession and teacher training. Your child needs the best, researched teaching practices implemented on a consistent basis.

Based upon my training, I expected my daughter to have these researched, educational experiences. I thought as a fellow educator, I would be told information that supported my teacher training. But much of the advice I was receiving seemed to be based on teachers' opinions rather than the researched educational practices.

I have heard teachers say, "You do not understand *special* education." It took me years to realize that researched educational practices apply to *all* children. My daughter's brain function, as well as her need for emotional support and a supportive community, do not diminish because she has special needs. In fact, she needs an extra-quality education. I think this must have been the definition of "special" when the supports were first created. After all, according to START special education was not designed to replace the general education curriculum. Special education was designed to give children access to the learning that takes place in the general curriculum.

Instead of this extra-quality education, general education teachers are often looking for someone else to work with these children—someone with more expertise. It is true that special educators receive additional training to support learning. But taken away from the general education and the social supports, special education fails. It is the role of the general education teacher to recognize the learning needs of the child and to work *with* the special education teachers and the staff providing supportive services. It is the role of the special education teacher to work *with* the general education teacher to support the learning needs of the child. It is within the context of the authentic learning environment where the child will have the supports and the desire to be included and succeed.

A great burden is placed on a child when skills are taught in isolation (down the hall in another room) and the child is expected to transfer the skills to a different learning environment. What benefit are skills taught away from their natural environments or away from the context of learning?

I know as a teacher that when my students left my classroom for special education services, I continued with my classroom lessons. (This is called a pull-out program.) When the children returned from the special education room, I had no idea what they had learned or how their learning transferred to my classroom.

I also taught at a school where the special education teacher came into my room. (This is called a push-in program.) She worked with a variety of students in the classroom. I saw her as a valuable resource to my teaching.

In the "pull-out" program, where the children left the room, I was told to schedule the "less important" lessons so that they would not miss as much from my classroom instruction. I always found this a little insulting. I never thought I had times of unimportance in my daily schedule. In my opinion, whenever the children left the room, they were missing my well-crafted lessons.

The No Child Left Behind legislation enacted by the Bush administration requires schools to be accountable for measurable performance for all children. Within that law, there is a nationwide movement to implement Response to Intervention (RTI). In the RTI guideline, a student that is struggling in school receives additional interventions based upon the individual child's needs. The interventions are often individual or small group lessons aimed at meeting the specific needs of the child. General education teachers rely on their knowledge of the student's needs and the curriculum to create these interventions. They implement best teaching practices. In the past, if the child's IQ score showed a wide discrepancy from their classroom performance, then the child could possibly be labeled "learning disabled." Instead educators now follow students' responses to their interventions to guide them in forming their opinions—with the hope of decreasing the disproportionate amount of children that are currently labeled as learning disabled. The data from the interventions are used to help people decide whether or not a child has learning disabilities.

I am confident that no one will be wondering if Marissa needs extra assistance. However, the climate of learning created in the classroom by RTI is a natural place to meet the needs of all children—especially children with special needs. Marissa needs a teacher that is ready to differentiate their instruction to meet Marissa's IEP goals. If done well, the classroom teacher will find the suggestions of Marissa's support staff helpful for creating interventions for other children in the class.

Therefore the way a child gets labeled learning disabled has changed. General education teachers must now document general education supports put in place to help students. It is the lack of progress over years that will allow a child to be considered for a label of having a learning disability. Therefore, teachers must differentiate instruction and teach all students. If the child requires greater supports, then they move up on the "tier" of supports needed. Other teachers may help with the implementation of additional supports and lessons.

In order to support RTI and to offer greater services to all students, some school districts want to blur the line between general education and special education. They want to have everyone working together to support all students. This is exactly what all students need—quality teaching.

In my teacher training, I learned not to have preconceived ideas about the learning potential of my students. I was trained to figure out the strengths of my students and use their strengths to bring their learning along. If I had concerns about a student, I brought in an expert to give ideas and to meet with parents to build a team of support for their child.

I want my daughter to have access to these rich learning experiences. Yet every year I feel like I am asked at IEP meetings essentially if I am ready to give up on my daughter's potential. Do I agree she needs a separate special education in a separate program surrounded only by children with special needs? No, I do not.

Why would I want my child to be taken away from teachers that have been trained to get her to reach her potential? It is true she may not be writing at a fifth grade level in fifth grade. I understand that none of my students in the fifth grade will be at the same level. I am not going to give up on the entire school experience.

This is Marissa's only opportunity to have children her age speaking to her. This is the only year she has the opportunity to listen to fifth grade stories. General education teachers have the grade-level expertise and training to help her form typical, appropriate grade-level social interactions.

We spent several years and hundreds of thousands of dollars on supplemental therapies and educational experiences, only to learn that she needed to be in a general education classroom for our work to be meaningful. In my opinion, taking children with special needs away from typical children to work with adults or other children with special needs does not work.

It is very difficult for teachers to have too many children in one class with behavior problems or too many children with special learning needs. General education teachers know that children will be negatively influenced by poor behaviors. They know it is difficult to reach the needs of children when too many children need their help. So whose idea was it to create separate classes of only children with special needs? Tracking children and keeping them in separate settings was never the intent of special education.

General education teachers are trained to keep anecdotal records on students. This means they chart what the child does and then create learning experiences to support the child's needs. Marissa requires lessons presented with modifications. General education teachers make modifications daily as a part of their professional experience.

Children need appropriate models of behavior. When typical children are learning to talk, it is common knowledge they must be spoken to and be in a rich verbal environment. Use your common knowledge about child development and apply it to your own child.

As you make educational decisions for your child, take time to be educated using the current educational research.

Important Points to Remember

- General education classrooms are naturally multi-leveled and multi-skilled environments.

- Presume competence and the ability for the child to understand—only then will creative ways to instruct in reading, social skills, and classroom content be created.

- Quality, researched educational practices apply to *all* children.

- Your child needs the best, researched teaching practices implemented on a consistent basis.

- Often by the second grade, many children with special needs are in separate classrooms for children with special needs and may come as visitors to general education classes, or they are in separate schools entirely.

- It is not professional simply to report that a child is not responding to instruction. If the child does not respond to a lesson, then modifications are made based on the needs of the child and then tried again, and again, and possibly again.

- If you want your child included in the general education school, then you need to be educated. It should be common practice for you to go online and read about the recommendations being made for your child.

- General education teachers have the grade-level expertise and training to help form typical, appropriate grade-level social interactions for all children.

- This may be the first time that your child's teacher has been given the trust and the expectation to use their general education training to address your child's needs.

Chapter 8
Individualized Educational Plan

Since the very beginning of Marissa's educational career, it was clear that she was going to need extra supports in order for her to reach her full potential. Since Marissa had identified needs as an infant, her educational career was supported by the school district long before kindergarten.

Children with delayed skills or other disabilities are eligible for special services that are outlined in their individualized educational programs (IEPs) in public schools free of charge for families. This plan is reported and monitored on a government-regulated form. Everyone on the IEP team must meet yearly to update the plan. The passage of the Individuals with Disabilities Act (IDEA 2004) made parents of children with disabilities crucial members of their child's educational team.

> Children with delayed skills or other disabilities are eligible for special services that are outlined in their individualized educational programs (IEPs) in public schools free of charge for families.

Understanding how to access these services allows you to be an effective advocate for your child. The educational plan for your child must be clearly written in the IEP document. School districts are required to follow the plan written in the IEP. The more specific and thoughtful you make your child's plan, the better educational experience your child will have.

I have a love/hate relationship with the IEP. I feel like the IEP is a deficit model. This paperwork must be filled in completely and thoughtfully. It kind of reminds me of doing my taxes—line by line there is specific required information. I think it is sad that you need to first agree to what is wrong with your child. Every year, our IEP meeting for Marissa begins with someone reading the PLEP—the Present Level of Educational Performance. This is a very long narrative describing all the things Marissa cannot do. Then we move on to the test results. The testing shows she is delayed in all areas.

There is one line where we can write anything about her real life interests, her curiosity about her surroundings, and her sweet personality. There is no determined area to note the remarkable progress she has made since kindergarten.

There is a section to write the label given to her. When Marissa was one year old, I told our advocate I would not allow Marissa to be labeled. Maria explained she understood my feelings, but the label allowed the access to services. Therefore, when Marissa was young, she was labeled cognitively multiply impaired. In the fourth grade IEP meeting, the experts reported that the label that better suited her was autistic. This is another reason I believe separate programs are not good for children. I have learned that is not uncommon for the label to change. The school Marissa was sent to as a child was not the school for children with autism—it was the school for children with cognitive impairments. Since Marissa was

Labeling a child allows access to services.

in her general education school and her label changed, her educational surroundings did not drastically change. Some of her support staff changed. However, her IEP goals continued to be met in the general education setting.

Overall, the label you get should match the kinds of services you need. I believed that Marissa would have been better labeled as autistic from the very beginning. At one school for students with autism, I was told that the teachers with the most seniority picked their students first. This means the teachers with the least seniority were educating some of the most difficult students. Since I did not think that was a good placement for Marissa, I agreed to the cognitively multiply impaired label in order to get Marissa the appropriate services. However, in fourth grade, the autistic label gave her access to more qualified occupational therapists and speech therapists that were better suited to address her needs in the general education classroom.

It is important that you tell your IEP team that you are agreeing to the label to support your child. However, kindly explain that you need staff members to use "people-first" language when talking about your child. This is a term you can research. You are asking for your child to be recognized as a person before their disability. Marissa is our daughter, a classmate, a neighbor, and a friend. If a reference must be made, she is a "child with disabilities." It is not respectful to call her a "disabled child." While there is some debate around the phrasing, I have found this to be the clearest way for people in school to understand that you are asking for your child to receive opportunities that other children their age are receiving.

> You are asking for your child to be recognized as a person before their disability.

> Stay focused on your child's limitless potential.

You will create the vision of your child as a person deserving the respect to be recognized and educated within their community. Teachers need to be told that you expect your child will go to college. You may want to practice saying this with conviction before you go into a meeting. You have probably been told many times there is little hope for your child. People that first encounter me think I am in denial of Marissa's disabilities. I am not. However, I stay focused on Marissa's limitless potential for developing her abilities.

I have found that it is critical to embrace Marissa as she is. She does not need to be "fixed" prior to entering school. I think many people have the misconception that children must learn a set of skills and then enter school. Children with disabilities have an IEP plan to support their needs. They should be in school to learn, not kept out of school until the learning happens. Marissa is perfect as she is. However, as perfect as I believe all of my children are, it does not mean that I do not expect them to grow and learn. I want Marissa, as all my children, to reach her greatest potential. I do not know what that is, and no one else should pretend to know her potential. We have all heard of someone that was given three months to live, and the person survived. I have heard about people learning to talk when they are in their twenties and then telling all the stories they remember from childhood.

Familiarize yourself with the Higher Educational Opportunity Act of 2008. In this law, there are new provisions that expand post-secondary education for students with intellectual disabilities. These students will be eligible for Pell Grants, along with Supplemental Educational Opportunity Grants and the Federal Work-Study Program. This law authorizes the expansion of high-quality, inclusive models of comprehensive transition and post-secondary programs. It ensures equal college opportunities for students with intellectual disabilities. I believe since your child has the possibility to be welcomed into college, your child should be permitted to attend grades K–12.

I think a big problem with the special education law is that extra services that your child is entitled to receive cost the school district money. I have learned that two of the most costly expenses in education are operating buildings and bussing. I think since school districts have budgets, they often do not tell you everything that is truly available to your child. It seems that some services are offered to some families that are not offered to others because one family has fought harder for it. You need to decide if services you may request are being denied because they do not think they will benefit your child, or if they are trying to save money. They will not tell you.

I often wondered why kids with the same labels are often grouped together in separate special education classes. Children with disabilities are all different. It is the IEP team that decides where the education of the

> Before attending an IEP meeting, you must have help with creating meaningful educational goals for your child.

child occurs. Remember, special education is not a place—it is a service. Before attending an IEP meeting, you must have help with creating meaningful educational goals for your child. You should get help from any outside therapists your child sees. Simply ask, "My child's IEP is soon. Do you have a few ideas for the IEP goals?" Also tell your advocate your hopes and dreams for your child. The advocate may have some good ideas for goals for your child.

If you want your child fully included, you must make sure most of the IEP goals are best achieved in the general education class. Putting Marissa in a separate class to "learn to talk" is probably not a reasonable goal for her. She has low muscle tone, and the muscles in her face impact her ability to speak. However, I want her to learn to communicate. Having communication goals in a general education classroom allows her many opportunities for success. She is learning a variety of formal and informal ways to communicate and she has many peers to truly interact with, and her IEP goals support this.

> If you want your child fully included, you must make sure most of the IEP goals are best achieved in the general education class.

I believe Marissa will learn more if she stays in the general curriculum. Some years the IEP does not reflect the small skills I hoped she would learn. However, every year she learns things that cannot be measured by goals in the IEP. By being with her peers, she has learned many natural lessons in friendship, laughter, fashion, popular culture, turn taking, and appropriate behavior. I believe this teaches people in the community that she belongs. In addition, since she is in the general education classroom, she is exposed to the general education curriculum.

According to the IEP, your child's goals are to be reviewed yearly, but anyone on the team at any time may call for an IEP meeting. You should try to honor everyone's time and not hold an IEP meeting more than once a year.

Everyone on your child's educational team will be invited to the IEP meeting. There are usually about ten staff members at meetings for Marissa. There is the physical therapist, speech therapist,

> Within the IEP, parents and educators will work together to write educational goals.

principal, occupational therapist, autism consultant, special education director, inclusion consultant, social worker, classroom teacher, our advocate, and us. We have been told it takes a lot of time and money to coordinate everyone's schedules.

Within the IEP, parents and educators will work together to

write educational goals. Technically, the goals are supposed to be written together at the meeting. However, do your homework before the meeting. Ask your advocate and your child's therapists for ideas for reasonable, achievable goals in the general education setting. I often send an email to the staff members with a list of goals I would like to be considered for Marissa's IEP so that when we meet our time can be used to discuss them. Within the IEP document, you also agree to the needed supports and the amount of time they will spend providing service to your child.

You need to enter the IEP in the spirit of working together—cooperating. If you disagree with someone, you need to politely explain how to re-word their suggestion if possible. Once in a while, I encounter someone that gives me the feeling they do not want Marissa at "their" school and it seems they try to sabotage my efforts.

I have been at an IEP meeting where someone said, "We cannot do that because our union will not allow it." I see this as a creative way of saying they do not want a child with special needs in "their" general education class. However, this is a *public* school and my daughter is a member of the public. I know that every day teachers address the varied needs of children related to gender, race, religion, and learning disabilities.

> You need to enter the IEP in the spirit of working together.

Of course I was sad and disappointed the teacher wasn't conveying their excitement to educate my sweet daughter. Yes, my heart was broken. But this is not about me. I need to remain professional in order to allow my daughter to have the opportunities to succeed in school. People will say things that surprise you. Just remember to keep your child's best interests in the forefront of your mind.

If you are organized and you have clearly communicated your needs, your meeting will hopefully go smoothly. Do not wait until the IEP meeting to voice any concerns you have. You should be working on solving problems that arise on a daily basis.

Talk to your advocate ahead of time about what you hope to achieve in the meeting. If a disagreement arises that makes you feel uncomfortable, you have the right to adjourn the meeting. Since so many people have arranged to be there on your child's behalf, try not to do this unless you feel it is necessary. If you have a question that you do not want to discuss in front of the group, simply ask for the group to take a five-minute break so you may talk with your advocate privately.

Keep your child's best interests in the forefront of your mind.

Do not wait until the IEP meeting to voice any concerns you have.

Within the meeting, you should discuss where the supports will take place. Ideally, I would like Marissa to receive all her supports in the classroom. This means I would like the support teachers to come into the classroom and help to develop communication skills in the classroom environment. Educating in an inclusive setting is new to many support teachers. Many support teachers do not talk about team teaching and being effective in a group setting. Therefore, this has been an area where I have needed to compromise.

I think that having an IEP meeting more than once a year only allows more opportunities for your child to be removed from the general education setting. Once our paperwork is signed, I try to leave this document alone. However, there have been some years where everything has fallen apart for Marissa at school.

One year, people told us that the support staff was unkind to Marissa and some support staff stopped showing up as scheduled. I sought the advice of a kind-hearted educator that I have known since Marissa was a baby. He understands the art of compromise and getting things done. He suggested that I "go up the food chain" until I found someone

that would help me. Always try to resolve your concerns first with the classroom teacher. They should be the primary contact person. As a teacher, I found it annoying if a parent went to the principal without speaking to me first. If you are still not happy after talking with the classroom teacher, then approach the principal and ask for help for your child. Inquire about what can be done to get support for your child and the teacher. Only in desperate times have I sought help above the principal. There are usually people hired to be in charge of principals. I think you need to remain focused on your goal—you want your child to be successful in school. You are on a loving mission for the implementation of your child's IEP. If you have a complaint, it needs to be directly linked to your child's IEP document.

I like using email because it gives a written record of our communications. Just remember that anything you write in an email is probably forwarded to all the IEP team members. I have been asked to state my concerns by explaining my own worries and feelings so I am not slandering anyone's reputation. In addition, as frustrated as you may get, you must try to remain professional, which can be difficult to do when your sweet child seems to be suffering.

If people are not following the IEP, the district will be out of compliance, in which case, there are legal steps that you can take. You will need to carefully document all incidents and involve a special education attorney to help you.

I have consulted with an attorney when Marissa's program was not being implemented. He clearly told me that every detail I wanted to happen at school must be documented in the IEP. Special education attorneys can give you advice without being brought in to take over your child's programming.

Often at the IEP meetings, someone will say, "Of course we'll do that; we do not need to write it." I reply, "I know you'll do it, but I'll feel better if it is written there."

Sometimes I need to meet with members of the IEP team, but I do not need the formal IEP meeting since I do not want to change any of the official forms. I just want people to implement what they agreed to do on the form.

I need to keep my goal in mind. My goal is to have Marissa graduate with her peers. My understanding is that once lawyers and mediators get involved you lose a lot of the IEP's flavor. We are supposed to be working as a team.

Do not assume the IEP plan is being carried out daily. You must follow through every day. Look at your child's daily reports and work. Does this reflect what you agreed to in the IEP?

In my teaching experience, it was common that every few years a parent requested to meet with me once a week or once a month to keep up on their child's progress. Usually teachers do not like doing this, but many will agree if you have a good reason.

You have been with your child for many years. Try to be clear in what you need for your child. However, do not expect people will be ready to fully hear your message the first time you meet.

You need to manage your time as a parent. You need to have efficient meetings. If you are managing the meetings, plus a child with special needs along with the needs of your family, you are probably coming to meetings with many worries. Try to stay very focused on the purpose of every meeting. I often write four or five

Try to stay very focused on the purpose of every meeting.

agenda points that I keep in front of me so I do not forget anything. I anticipate their questions and have information ready to give them. Always tell school personnel your purpose for meeting.

No one likes to be surprised at a meeting. If you are asked to attend a meeting, request very clear reasons why they want to meet with you. This will give you time to gather your thoughts and call your advocate if needed. You may also add a few things you would like to discuss. After all, all members of the IEP team are supposed to be working together.

Try to agree to an ending time to your meetings before the meeting begins. If the meeting is incomplete, you can agree to meet for a few more minutes or you can agree to schedule a follow-up meeting. Do not allow meetings to go much past the agreed-upon ending. You have work to do at home to support your child with special needs. There will always be time for another meeting.

After the IEP, I requested monthly meetings to keep track of Marissa's progress. They started out by monitoring her behavior. Now I am trying to change the focus to discussing Marissa's daily instruction. Like all kids, if she has good instruction, good behavior follows. I simply explain I need the meetings because

> Try to agree to an ending time to your meeting before the meeting begins.

"I want to keep up with my child's progress." I must keep my focus on Marissa. It is never in Marissa's best interest for me to get angry in front of teachers or members of the IEP team.

In every meeting you attend, you must bring and refer to your child's IEP goals. This is what drives your child's instruction. In September, I usually type the goals and give the teacher and the paraprofessionals copies. If not, I find the months go by and people are unclear of what Marissa is supposed to be doing at school. If you are unhappy with something happening at school, you must find the link to the IEP goal.

Schools are mostly run by women. It may be beneficial to have a man attend every meeting with you. If you are not married, possibly your brother or your father can attend meetings with you. I have found

It is never in your child's best interest to get angry in front of teachers or members of the IEP team.

that having the voice of a man in the room can change the tone of the meeting. My husband is not an educator so usually he lets me do most of the talking. However, once in a while he voiced a few comments as Marissa's daddy—it was clear she was loved by many and it showed we were united in helping our daughter receive an education.

Teachers usually express concern over time. They worry that educating Marissa will take too much of their time. If they try to keep Marissa educated throughout the day away from her peers, then this will take a great amount of time.

If you are unhappy with something happening at school, you must find the link to the IEP goal.

However, if teachers welcomed her support staff in to assist them and applied successful adaptations to many lessons, this would be very manageable.

In 2005, the Michigan State Board of Education approved the Vision and Principals of Universal Design as a framework and foundation for policy development. This gives educators a framework for meeting all students' needs. Including my daughter in school is not a new idea I created. I am fortunate there are policies supporting my work. I am thankful for the work of the parents that have come before me. Sadly, I have met mothers that experienced the same resistant attitudes twenty years ago when they helped their own children through their neigh-borhood schools.

I met a mother of a grown son with disabilities who offered me wonderful advice. She looked at my worried, tired face and said, "Enjoy your daughter. My son is now twenty-six, and I did not take the time to enjoy his childhood. I was so worried about school; the time flew by."

One of the wonderful things about being Marissa's mother is that I have met many wonder-ful, kind-hearted, loving people. Marissa connects me to people in a beautiful, loving way that I would have missed if I was not blessed to be her mother. I have met educators that embrace the challenge of meeting Marissa's needs and celebrate her successes. While our focus is on Marissa, it is wonderful knowing that her presence makes the world more meaningful and beautiful for the children she is with.

Remember to enjoy your child.

I feel blessed to be Marissa's mother.

Embrace the challenges and celebrate the successes.

Important Points to Remember

- The Individuals with Disabilities Act (IDEA 2004) made parents of children with disabilities crucial members of their child's educational team.

- Children with delayed skills or other disabilities are eligible for special services that are outlined in their individualized educational programs (IEPs) in public schools free of charge for families.

- In September, type the goals listed on your child's IEP document and give copies to your child's teacher and paraprofessionals.

- Gather ideas for IEP goals you would like for your child prior to attending the IEP meeting.

- All the equipment, supports, and services that your child requires must be clearly written on the IEP document along with your child's goals.

- Bring your advocate to every meeting.

- It may be helpful for you to request a short break during a meeting in order to discuss something with your advocate.

- The label your child receives gives your child the access to all the supports and services they will need at school in order to be successful.

- If you are unhappy with something happening at school, you must find the link to the IEP goal.

- You will create the vision of your child as a person deserving the respect to be recognized and educated within their community.

Chapter 9
Discrimination

I have learned that including a child with disabilities in the world unfortunately is not the norm. Therefore, many people have not had a lot of experience with people with disabilities. We have also met people that did not value Marissa in the world. I have experienced discrimination that I did not believe existed before holding the hand of a child with a disability.

One day I went to visit my favorite aunt, Margaret, who is ninety-five years old. I exclaimed, "Aunt Margaret, when I take Marissa to school, some of the mothers actually frown at me and look harshly at Marissa."

She stopped me and explained, "You are a wonderful mother. Hold your head up high. You are doing a noble job." I hear her message when I encounter difficult people.

One year there was a member of Marissa's IEP team that seemed to have difficulties. I felt it would be more beneficial if this person weren't on Marissa's IEP team, so I requested to have that person removed. I have learned that one person working against the team creates a terrible working climate. In addition, the behavioral data indicated our daughter was very distressed in her presence. However, in the spirit of cooperation, we agreed to continue to work to educate the team member.

This was not the first time I was concerned about the people working with Marissa. In a previous year, Marissa had arrived home for a few weeks in a row with unexplained bruises. From that point on, we all agreed that any bruises from school must come with an explanation of what happened.

On a Sunday afternoon, I watched Marissa walk up three concrete steps to our back door. Right in front of me, she fell backward down the stairs. I felt terrible. Overall, she was fine. She had three small bruises on her side from the fall. I think I felt sadder than she did. However, I was unprepared for the next events that would bring me even greater sadness.

Before school on Monday, I called to assure the people at school that I would not think the bruises happened there. I explained witnessing her falling on the steps outside our home.

After school on Tuesday, I took the children outside to play at home. My neighbor came over and we talked while we watched the children play. I had not checked the answering machine. While the children were playing, my husband called. He explained that he had been in a meeting all afternoon and had just checked his voicemail. He told me he just received several urgent messages from someone at Child Protective Services. The woman from Child Protective Services seemed to know a lot about our family. She knew the names of our children and where they went to school. He told me that he returned her call and left her an urgent message. He wanted to know exactly who she was and why she was calling.

I could feel my face turning pale as I looked at my neighbor in our backyard. I asked her to watch the children while I went inside to check our answering machine. We had indeed received a message from Child Protective Services. The woman sternly explained that she needed to speak with my husband and me immediately. Since it was already five o'clock on Tuesday, she explained she would see us in her office at eight the next morning. She told us to bring a copy of Marissa's IEP with us to the meeting.

My husband and I later learned that our seven-year-old son had been pulled from his first grade class and interviewed by an investigator from Child Protective Services. We learned the investigator had also met Marissa and asked the paraprofessionals questions.

I did not sleep the entire night. I wondered how this could be happening to our family. Why was a stranger demanding to meet with us about our children?

The next day, we kept our children home from school. We were worried that if we sent them to school, they may not come home. We paid a babysitter to stay with them.

My husband and I dressed in our most professional clothes. We gathered medical records and therapy receipts to show the work we do for Marissa. And of course, we brought a copy of her IEP document.

We drove to the Child Protective Services office. We arrived early. A stern-looking woman dressed in jeans and a t-shirt led us to a small room that had a one-way mirror and a small stainless steel table.

It became clear that misinformation had been given to CPS. There was not simply a report that I had called the school to report that Marissa had fallen on the steps at home.

The report stated that Marissa had rope marks on her back. Marissa was in "the wrong placement" at school. Marissa came to school dirty daily. I sent my daughter to school for a field trip without the proper outer gear. I sent her to school with a "no-care" attitude.

I was horrified. As all mothers, I took pride in being a great mother to my children. But as a mother of a child with special needs, I had been even more diligent in attending to her needs before sending her off to school. I took extra care to protect her from the eyes of judgment. These were statements about my sweet daughter. I dressed her in beautiful, fashionable clothes with carefully brushed hair. This was my sweet child, for whom I had spent countless hours in classes and in meetings to prepare the way for a wonderful education for her. The child that came to school daily with homemade lunches. The child that had been taken across the country to meet with specialized doctors and participated in countless therapy sessions. The child with "that mother" who demanded all her daughter's educational needs be met in the general education classroom. I couldn't believe this was happening.

We learned that, based on the report, they were prepared to pull all three of our children from our care immediately. We learned that because Marissa is non-verbal, this went all the way to the top. However, the investigator explained that once she got to school and started interviewing people, she realized the report did not match what everyone else in the school was saying about our family. In addition, the school personnel had informed the staff at Child Protective Services that we were good parents. Luckily the investigation saved us from the agony of being in court, fighting to get our children returned to our custody.

No one from the school would tell us who made the report because reports to Child Protective Services are confidential.

We made a police report to recover pictures that were taken of our daughter's back (while all the students were in the classroom). We went to the board of education office and requested that the person who reported the misinformation about our family immediately be removed from any interactions with our children at school. We found this report so unusual and bizarre that we were worried about our safety. We also insisted on more training on inclusive teaching practices.

We met with an attorney. He was interested in taking our case to help create laws to protect people that are falsely accused.

Make sure the people working with your child have your child's best interests at heart.

Based on the report, we think Child Protective Services should have investigated. We were fortunate the investigator was skilled in uncovering the truth—that we were good parents to our children.

We have learned you cannot change people's prejudices. Make sure the people working with your child have your child's best interests at heart. I do not demand a certain teacher for my child. If the teacher does not want to be Marissa's teacher, then I do not want it either.

Be aware of how people are viewing your interactions with your child. Unfortunately, you need to protect your child from the prejudices and discrimination that come with having a disability.

I need to be aware of how to protect our family now and in the future. The next several months I had nightmares of people trying to take my children from me. As a mother of a child with disabilities, this was an incredible hardship.

We believed another discriminatory experience was one summer we heard that parents were asked if they would mind if their child would be in Marissa's class the next year. If the parent minded, then the child would not be placed with Marissa. As a teacher, I honored the confidentiality of my students. School personnel should never discuss someone else's child. I believe this sent the message that essentially the parents had the right to discriminate against our child with a disability.

Unfortunately, you will probably recognize the harsh look of unacceptance from some parents you see at school. Usually these brief disapproving looks are at Marissa when the adult thinks I'm not looking. However, look beyond their faces and you will see faces of other parents that exhibit such love, kindness, and acceptance that your heart will melt.

Important Points to Remember

- Be aware of how people are viewing your interactions with your child.

- It is against the law to file a false report to Child Protective Services.

- Request staff and community training about the importance of inclusion of all students in school.

- Remember to hold your head up high. You are working in the best interests of your child.

Chapter 10
Behave or Else

We teach our children to strive for the American dream—if we work hard enough, we can be anything we want to be. In our spiritual faith, we teach our children that with God all things are possible.

Since we are living a faith-based American life, we believe that Marissa, like all our children, has unlimited potential that is truly unknown to us. This is the joy of being their parents. We guide them and they respond to our teachings in unexpected ways.

We believe Marissa needs to be educated. Sometimes in school, we feel like people judge Marissa harshly for her perceived lack of skills or knowledge.

I believe that instead of saying, "Look what *Marissa* doesn't know," we should say, "Look what *we* have not yet taught her." I think that anyone that points a finger to judge her should turn the finger around and point it at themselves.

It seems that people often try shifting the educational responsibility to someone else. However, everyone needs to use their training and work with others to create something more wonderful than anyone could do on their own. This takes collaboration and meetings.

As Marissa's parents, we expect meetings about the best ways to instruct Marissa. We expect to hear about the best practices being used for teaching her to read and learn math. However we have never received an urgent phone call to discuss Marissa's learning. Information about Marissa's learning seems to come up in conversations as secondary information. The primary focus of most of our conversations with staff members is focused around Marissa's behaviors. The biggest and most serious concerns arise because of her behavior.

While Marissa can make vocalizations and yell, she cannot speak. Due to her low muscle tone and difficulty with coordination, she was not able to learn sign language as a young child. Eventually, Marissa gained enough muscle tone in her body to begin learning the Picture Exchange Communication System (PECS), but she does not have enough experience with this to rely on it to meet all her needs.

How did Marissa let us know we were on our way to being reported to Child Protective Services? Marissa communicated in the most efficient way she could—through her behavior. She sat on the floor (the staff called this behavior "dropping"). She yelled. She tried to get away. She refused to do the work.

At our meetings, the staff reported that Marissa was not acting "appropriately," and she was disturbing the learning of others. They were "very concerned about Marissa's placement." In other words, they were letting us know that we needed to figure out a way to make her behave or they were going to send her away from the inclusive setting to a more "appropriate" (separate) placement. After all, they told us, she was not allowed to disturb the learning of others.

We lived with this fear for years. We sent Marissa to school in the morning, and we prayed during the day for her to behave.

One afternoon, we received a call from school. The person said, "You need to come get Marissa. She is not wearing her shoes. The rule is she must wear shoes. Since she is not wearing shoes, she must go home."

Instantly I panicked. Many thoughts raced through my mind. Marissa needed to be engaged in reading and math activities. She needed to learn to communicate with her peers. She was being sent home because she was not wearing her shoes?

I had no idea how to get Marissa to keep her shoes on. How long would I have to keep her home? This was not a behavior I had any control over. This was a behavior that had been going on since preschool.

I simply said that I would come to pick her up from school.

I felt desperate. As I looked for my car keys, I called our advocate. I frantically asked, "What should I do? They just called me from school telling me to come get Marissa."

Our advocate calmly replied, "Don't go get her yet. Stop at the board of education office first and request the policy that states that a child must wear shoes at school. There probably isn't such a policy. But if there is, then we need to meet to make an IEP goal for her that addresses that policy."

The advocate responded to the situation calmly and reasonably. As Marissa's mother, I was too emotionally attached to this sweet child to do this on my own. I appreciated her gentle voice of guidance.

I went right to the board of education office. I calmly introduced myself to the secretary, and I requested to speak to the person in charge of behavior policies. I explained that I wanted a copy of the shoe policy so I could write an IEP goal to support my daughter with special needs. My feelings of desperation were gone, and I now felt empowered to help Marissa.

I learned that indeed there was not a policy about wearing shoes. A director explained this could be classified under general safety policies. However, everyone agreed we probably did not need to amend the IEP to add the shoe-wearing goal. They agreed that Marissa's other goals could address this need. Indeed, Marissa could remain in school.

Marissa's inability to keep shoes on was related to her disability. This was not a "family problem." She needed the staff at the school to help her learn to tolerate shoes. Until this meeting, I had been trying to solve this issue (related to her disability) all by myself. I had been buying a variety of shoes and making excuses for her. Even praying that she would behave was not enough to make her wear her shoes.

Marissa had an IEP team of professionals to help her learn to do this. Parents should not feel responsible about something the child can learn at school. Over and over again, new behaviors came up. And over and over again, people wanted to label these "misbehaviors." Marissa had disabilities, and she needed to be taught how to behave, not punished.

I suddenly felt free of a great burden. No longer did I feel responsible to instantly "fix" her or feel like I had to try to hide her

Don't be part of the problem; be part of the solution.

disabilities. When issues were brought up, I could actually agree with school personnel. Even better, I could hold school personnel accountable for working with us to try to solve the behaviors.

One of the people on Marissa's IEP team had a wonderful phrase, "Don't be part of the problem; be part of the solution." She expected that anyone that brought a problem to the table should be ready with ideas on how to address the problem and create a solution.

At one of our meetings, I faced my fear of having Marissa sent away from our neighborhood school. I told school personnel that I agreed that Marissa should not be allowed to disturb the learning of others. However, I further explained that I did not think she should disturb the learning of general education students *or* special education students. Moving her to a different setting would not change her behaviors. It would just move her. In addition, a new school, away from her family and friends, would probably create more stress and create more undesirable behaviors. Most importantly, changing schools would not support one of her IEP goals of "being socially interactive with her peers." I was tired of feeling threatened that Marissa's behavior would determine where she would go to school, rather than her needs that were clearly described in her IEP.

I asked the school staff to consider what they were saying about the learning needs of the class of children they proposed she join in a separate special education room. Do children with disabilities have fewer rights than general education students? I think the reaction of many general education teachers is to "send them" (students with special needs) somewhere else. I think the general education teachers should go and see where these children end up. Then they should carefully consider if they would allow their own child to be placed away from their friends and neighbors.

A separate school would not "heal" her. Marissa would have disabilities wherever we placed her. The problem of disturbing others needed to be addressed. Just because students have been placed in a separate setting does not mean they can tolerate being interrupted. I believe Marissa would receive better models of appropriate behavior in the general education setting.

I changed how I approached the issue of behavior. Instead of getting defensive and alarmed, I instead asked, "So how are you going to help her with this?"

There should not be blame placed on the child or on you for behaviors related to your child's disability. We are asking the school personnel to teach our children every aspect of learning. Do not take their accusations of your child personally. Simply ask them kindly, "How are you going to help her learn to do this?"

> When an issue arises, ask the teacher, "How are you going to help my child with this?"

It is important to figure out why your child is exhibiting these behaviors. Luckily the autism consultant explained that "all behavior is communication." For example, Marissa started tossing things when she was done with them. Marissa needed to learn to put things on the desk or in a basket when she was done. She would knock something over during a difficult lesson. The staff needed to learn that Marissa would try to distract them in order to get out of doing something difficult.

Most importantly, listen to your child's appeal for help. I knew from my experience at the separate school that Marissa's pale, sad face told me that something was terribly wrong. Just because you send your child to a specific program does not mean that the most qualified person will be with your child. We sent Marissa to the separate school with the "highest qualified" teacher to meet her needs. Marissa came home with her shoes duct taped to her feet.

A plan for your child's behavior must be created. It is my hope that the general education teachers see

> You need to be the voice of unwavering support for your child. You can help the staff think through issues, but do not try to take them over.

themselves routinely collaborating with special education teachers rather than looking for the instructions on how to approach a child with special needs. It is my hope that as common practice, general education teachers feel empowered to use their years of experience to find creative ways to include students with disabilities in their daily lessons.

You need to be the voice of unwavering support for your child. You can help the staff think through issues, but do not try to take them over. You have asked the staff to support your child. Expect them to do their jobs.

Sometimes parents request their outside consultants to work

with the school personnel. The only way the district pays for a specific consultant, service, or program is when your child has a need that the district does not already cover. Indeed, they can agree to bring in an outside person or program, but this may be difficult to obtain since this is an expense to them.

We have paid for outside behavioral support for Marissa. Usually the school personnel will agree to observations from an outside person if you explain that you are trying to bridge the learning between school and home, and you are willing to pay for the consultant. We paid the behavioral consultant $100 an hour. After all, she figured out how to get Marissa to wear shoes.

The behavioral consultant told us to buy high-top tennis shoes for Marissa. She instructed us to put them on Marissa and have her practice walking around the block for an entire weekend. She told us that Marissa would fuss, but she needed to learn to get used to wearing shoes. She told us to let the teacher know that Marissa would be wearing new shoes on Monday. We practiced all weekend.

Monday morning, I took Marissa to school. I couldn't believe I was leaving my child at the door throwing a temper tantrum. I greeted the paraprofessional, gave her Marissa's hand, and told her, "Don't take off her shoes." I left feeling hopeful that our weekend shoe practice would pay off.

Still, I worried the entire day. I wondered how Marissa was doing. At the end of the day, I pulled the daily reporting sheet from her folder before we left the parking lot. The note said, "Marissa fussed for about thirty minutes and then did not fuss about the shoes for the rest of the day." After I read the report with Marissa, I told Marissa how proud I was of her for wearing her shoes for the entire day.

This year I attended autism educational training. The presenter began by telling us her name and said, "Now, we all know that taking off shoes and getting naked means, 'I'm not happy.' We're all past this, right?" The light went on inside my head that Marissa's actions of taking off her shoes was clear communication to us that she was unhappy about something.

The more difficult Marissa's behavior gets, the more I believe the adults around her are not implementing the goals of Marissa's IEP program. When Marissa's supports are not in place, she feels distressed and acts out.

> When Marissa's supports are not in place, she feels distressed and acts out.

My understanding of public school law is that schools are required to offer a range of services to students from "most restrictive" (separate schools) to "least restrictive" (inclusion) settings. I find this perplexing. To me, the educational research is clear that inclusive practices are best for all children.

I believe that one day historians will look back at the practice of separating students with special needs with a sense of disbelief.

> Whether your child is verbal or nonverbal, it is important that you see your child's behaviors as communicating their needs.

However, I do not have time for the educational system to evolve. I would not let a doctor perform surgery based on practices from thirty years ago. I cannot allow my daughter to be educated using old practices.

It is important that you see your child's behaviors as communicating their needs. On another occasion when Marissa's behavior reports came home negative, we again became concerned. It was not until a month later that we learned the expectation for the class had changed. They were expected to work more quietly. However, there had not been any changes to Marissa's program to prepare her for this.

I have not read any state curriculum requirements phrased as, "getting ready for the next grade." However, teachers seem to worry a lot about the opinions of the teacher in the next grade. It is most helpful to your child for the teacher to be very present-minded. I believe that quality daily teaching will naturally get children "ready for the next grade." Remember that the best teaching practices apply to all grades.

It is important to try to stay in touch with what is happening at school. One day, I saw a child being carried down the hall by two staff members. She was kicking, wiggling, and screaming, "I ain't wearing those shoes!" The one shoe she still had on flew up in the air. I walked over and picked up the brand new tennis shoe. I held the shoe and I realized there was another mother experiencing my agony. I followed the commotion into the office.

I explained to one of the staff members that the girl should be treated with more dignity than being carried all the way to the office.

The staff member seemed annoyed with me. She explained that she had been doing this "for years" and she knew what she was doing. I explained there were trained behaviorists that could be brought in to help with this. Do not accept practices that have been used "for years"—accept researched practices.

Be proactive in your child's education. If a new person needs to be hired, offer to be a part of the hiring committee. Staff members may refuse your input, but at least you have offered to help.

I did not understand that if we did not find a qualified person for a posted job position, it was possible to repost the position. Looking back, there was a time we probably should have reposted a position. It is worth the time to wait and select wonderful staff to support your child.

Shortly after the new person started working with my child, Marissa came home with the same look I had seen in the separate school—tired, sad, and pale. This is when I learned the importance of keeping data. Week by week, I charted Marissa's progress. Then, I requested a meeting with the principal. I showed her how much of a decline our daughter had made since the new person was hired to be with her. Marissa's behavior was the only way for her to communicate what was happening at school.

I was never told that my data made a difference. However, in time, the new personnel was moved to a different position. In this warm and friendly school, the unkindness toward our daughter stood out as unusual. While Marissa could not tell me what was happening, there were plenty of neighborhood children and their mothers telling me how distressed Marissa was at school. Her community was helping to keep her safe.

> Keep a journal of your child's progress. It can be useful for multiple reasons.

I no longer ask if a general education teacher has experience working with children with special needs. Instead I ask, "How does the teacher feel about inclusion?" In addition, just because a teacher requests your child does not mean this is the best match for your child.

You need a teacher that works well with others and can incorporate others into their school day. Marissa needed a teacher that could simply take someone's suggestion and implement it into her day.

As a parent, in this sometimes emotionally draining experience, I think it is important to develop grace. Volunteer to help in your child's classroom. Overlook the small things that may bother you. Look for the positive

> It is important to develop grace.

experiences and build on them. Tell the people that work with your child about the progress you see your child making. Acknowledge staff members for their successes with your child. Write letters of appreciation.

You are asking people to do things that are new to them. There will probably be many moments of frustration. But as you know, these moments only lead to greater satisfaction when things go well.

Facilitated communication is a method of holding a child's hand and helping them point to the letters of words they want to say. It seemed reasonable to us, so we started trying this with Marissa.

I don't know if facilitated communication will be her preferred way to communicate, but the message here is powerful. Just because Marissa does not speak, does not mean she does not understand. And if you believe it is *possible* she understands, she must be kept among people that will explain the world to her. Most importantly, she must be around her peers. Think back to when you were a child in school. Who did you learn from? Your peers.

I witnessed a child in a separate class for children with autism using facilitated communication to communicate to an *adult*. I do not expect Marissa to be doing "fifth grade school work," but I also do not expect her to spend most of her time interacting with adults. She can participate in fifth grade concepts and do her work as best as she physically can with her low muscle tone. Most importantly, she can communicate with other fifth grade students.

It is complicated. The person that may know the most about your child's disability in your school district may not have experience with successful inclusion experiences. Therefore, it is the integration of everyone's knowledge that makes inclusion work.

Marissa has difficulty with coordination. Before an adaptive physical education teacher was added to the general-education physical education class, Marissa received most of her instruction from a paraprofessional during physical education class.

I asked the physical education teacher if he ever instructed Marissa. I asked him if the paraprofessional could be used to occasionally instruct the general education students, so Marissa could also get the attention she needed from the physical education teacher.

The physical education teacher replied, "The other (general education) parents would not like their children being instructed by a paraprofessional rather than the teacher."

I said, "Yes, you are right. I do not want *my* child's physical education instruction coming only from a paraprofessional." I felt Marissa was worthy of the general education teacher's time too.

Paraprofessionals are not assigned to replace your child's teacher. They are assigned to assist your child within the daily instruction. Your child should be instructed and spoken to by the teacher.

After our meeting, the physical education teacher started giving Marissa more attention in class. In addition, a wonderful adaptive physical education teacher was added to work with the general education teacher during the class. The teachers worked wonderfully together to support all the students in the class. Physical education became one of Marissa's favorite classes. This is especially amazing because she has physical disabilities! I wrote letters of appreciation for the general education gym teacher and the new adaptive gym teacher.

I received an email reply from the general education gym teacher saying he was "happy to be doing his small part for Marissa's education"—this is exactly right. Everyone does a small part and therefore makes a huge positive impact on Marissa's educational experience.

We have a never-ending job. Children with special needs can be an easy target. The child should never be blamed for the mistakes of the adults in charge.

One year there was a long-term substitute teacher. We

> Everyone's small part makes a huge positive impact on a child's educational experience.

86

were told that the substitute teacher was instructed "not to worry about teaching Marissa." It seemed the administration expected the varied support staff to step in to be the "teacher" to Marissa while the general education teacher was away. Unlike the rest of the parents, we needed to accept that our daughter would not be under the constant watch of the substitute teacher. We trusted her support staff, so this was a compromise we made, knowing we must pick our battles carefully. However, this was very difficult for Marissa.

The last week of school, the teacher returned from her leave of absence. We did not tell her the sadness we experienced while she had been away. We were grateful for the time our daughter had with her.

Important Points to Remember

- If your child is having difficulty with a particular behavior at school, write an IEP goal to support your child's needs. This additional goal can simply be added as an amendment to the IEP document without the entire team coming together again.

- There should not be blame placed on the child or you for behaviors related to your child's disability.

- It is important that you see your child's behaviors as communicating their needs.

- Refrain from trying to micromanage what is happening at school for your child. Expect the school personnel to use their expertise to address your child's needs.

- Honor the teacher's time before and after school. Try to stay within the common communication systems, such as class notebooks and your child's communication devices. It is stressful for teachers to try to communicate daily with parents outside of the routine of their classrooms.

- Tracking behavioral data related to your child's IEP goals will let you know where your child needs more support.

- I believe that quality daily teaching will naturally get children "ready" for the next grade

- Quality teaching practices apply to all grades.

- Stay in touch with what is happening at school for your child.

- Offer to be on the hiring committee if new staff is being hired to work with your child.

Chapter 11
Addressing Medical Needs

It is shocking how much medication is routinely given out in the office of public schools. Parents send in medication for ADHD, asthma, headaches, and allergies. There are EpiPens and special tables for children with peanut allergies to eat their lunch. All of the medications have the potential for serious, adverse side effects. According to school district policy, a doctor's note and a parent signature is required for all medication.

When Marissa was nine years old, she started having seizures. On most days, Marissa's seizures were controlled with daily seizure medication. However, once a seizure began, she needed to be given medication to make the seizure stop.

At home, Marissa had received the emergency seizure medication over a hundred times. At school, she has only needed it once. One day the school nurse called to inform me that the school district personnel would no longer be administering the emergency seizure medication that I sent to school. The nurse explained they would wait for EMS to administer the medication.

I expressed my concern about relying on EMS arriving in a timely fashion when a seizure could be stopped immediately. I reminded her they had a doctor's note and our signature. The nurse understood my worry and shared my concern with meeting Marissa's needs. A short time later, she called me back and said, "Marissa's medical plan will remain the same. She will receive medication at the onset of a seizure." I was grateful that the nurse took the time to thoughtfully support our daughter's needs.

I know some people want schools for children with special needs because of medical issues that often accompany having special needs. Yet children with medical needs routinely attend general education schools. For example, a child in a general education school who has a severe peanut allergy is medically at risk if exposed to peanut products. We do not send that child to a school with only other children with peanut allergies.

> It is important to have a medical plan for your child.

Children need to learn how to manage their medical issues as they live in the community. Having medication with them and/or available to them is one of the responsibilities they will have.

It is important to have a medical plan for your child. This allows the staff to feel confident and capable in working with your child. You are with your child daily. Chances are you do not have a medical degree. Someone trained you or you have hired medical staff to assist you. You will need to work with the school to create a medical plan for your child.

Important Points to Remember

- Children with medical needs routinely attend general education schools.

- Children need to learn how to manage their medical issues as they live in the community.

- Knowing that your child is among well-trained staff will give you the freedom to address the other needs of your family while your child is at school.

Chapter 12
Surviving vs. Thriving

There are days when being a parent seems impossible. How am I supposed to accomplish everything I need to in order to make my children successful? As my children's mother, I am responsible for helping to shape happy, well-adjusted, independent adults. Therefore, I give them a strong spiritual faith to anchor them. I make sure they are well educated. I help them with their homework and read with them at home. I model healthy eating habits and cook healthy meals. I enroll them in sports. I talk with them about their relationships. I pass down the family traditions and lessons I have learned. I do all of this in hope of making their lives a little better than my own.

I have become aware that my children are watching me. More than my daily lessons, they are looking to me as a model of how to live their lives. I have a child with special needs, and great demands have been placed on me. Regardless of what I have been given, I am supposed to be a model of an adult living a well-adjusted, happy life.

In addition to the typical day-to-day activities of homework and extracurricular activities, I have the physical and emotional stress of knowing that my eleven-year-old daughter is very dependent on my decisions for her success in the world. Regardless of my parenting at home, my two sons will be welcomed at their neighborhood school and participate in typical activities without much effort from me. A few poor school meetings for Marissa, and my desire to have her in her neighborhood school may be thwarted.

As with all mothers, there are weeks I think I am doing a fabulous job. Then there are weeks I feel less effective. It is important for mothers of children with special needs to remember that being a mother is a difficult job. We are not alone.

> Remember that being the mother of a child with special needs is a difficult job.

I need Marissa to have a skilled, organized teacher. She also needs a skilled, organized mother. Marissa is making me a better person. There are many days I feel like I am failing. I look around my home and think, "What happened?" The house is a mess, we have eaten out more times in a week than I would ever admit, and we are looking through the clean, unfolded laundry hoping to find the other sock.

My mother has identified these weeks. She walks into my house and says, "How much did the burglars take?"

If you have seen the show *Friends,* there is a character on the show, Monica, who resembles me before having three children. She is orderly. Everything has a sense of belonging and organization. However, what I didn't know about Monica was that she had a secret that was revealed in one episode. She had a closet that was hiding all the miscellaneous items that were not out in the open.

I think children with special needs thrive in environments that are orderly and predictable. Our lives run smoother when we can find things. On many days, my best hopes of organization are to get things put away and have a few "Monica closets." I also notice I have some Monica cupboards and drawers. I am constantly trying to keep up or catch up with the daily housework. Being able to find things and live in a clutter-free home makes everyone feel lighter.

On my busy days, I do not blame my lack of organization on having a child with special needs. I know I will best support my child with special needs in an environment of order. It is not a particular event that causes me to lose my organization. It is the weeks when I get hit with a series of stressful and unexpected events that I lose my way. Having to attend many appointments is stressful. If you have other children, you often need to arrange childcare and meals around appointments. In addition, it is emotionally challenging to move to different meetings about your child with special needs. You are meeting different people that have varied roles in your child's life. In addition, these people have their own personalities and opinions about your child that you are managing.

I used to go through weeks like this one thinking, "Oh no! What will I do? Look at my messy house, how can I take care of everything?"

I now look at a stressful week and think, "Here we go again." I notice the mess more as a scientist. I glance around and think, "Yes, this is a stressful week." I walk over the mess without an ounce of guilt. I know the wave of events will eventually calm down, and I will be able to attend to the details of my life again.

> I know the wave of events will eventually calm down, and I will be able to attend to the details of my life again.

Here is an example of a week that caused me to lose my organization. I had a hint this may be one of those stressful weeks because we had more than two school meetings scheduled in one week.

Monday: Worry turns into relief

We figured out that my mother can watch our three children successfully for about two hours. Therefore, on Monday night, we asked my mother to come and watch the children so my husband and I could attend Marissa's parent-teacher conference together. We had been having monthly meetings with school personnel, but this was our opportunity to hear from her general education teacher about Marissa's progress.

The week before our conference, the autism support teacher told us she would also be attending the conference with the general education teacher. As they spoke to us, it was clear that modifications were being made to the lessons so Marissa could be included in the general education class. They even took time to give Marissa a report card with grades that correlated with her special education progress report. My heart jumped as I thought, "This is a beautiful parent-teacher conference."

Both teachers reported that Marissa liked to independently use math graphing games on the computer. They each reported seeing this separately. We were thrilled to hear about Marissa enjoying curriculum content—and now we had two teachers telling us.

We were only briefly surprised that the principal also joined the meeting. Since we expected a parent-teacher conference, this was a brief moment of confusion for us. However, the principal had been a wonderful source of support for us as we worked to help our daughter. She seemed proud of the teachers' work and also celebrated Marissa's accomplishments. We left the conference feeling like our dreams of a meaningful education were coming true for our daughter.

Tuesday: Relief and happiness turn into worry

Today was the first meeting with the middle school personnel. Since we requested a meeting, we were invited to come to the middle school.

This middle school meeting took place in the afternoon while our children were at school. As my husband and I walked into the building, I told him that it felt like Marissa's preschool assessment was happening again. Were we really there to talk about middle school? Or would the people waiting to meet us have a completely different agenda?

We were greeted with handshakes and the formality of people we did not yet know. They wanted to make sure we understood that middle school was a big transition. It was a fast-paced and intense curriculum. The day was highly structured. They explained that middle school was much different than elementary school and that we needed to understand the ramifications of the middle school experience.

I presented them with a list of people, services, and supplies that would be necessary for Marissa's instruction. They explained that my husband and I needed to schedule a meeting to speak with the special education director. After we met with her on our own, then they would schedule another meeting with us.

I went to school early to pick up Marissa. I needed a few minutes to regroup and to get some fresh air after our meeting. The happiness and excitement from the parent-teacher conference had left me. I felt like I should be experiencing the relief of Marissa completing elementary school. However, now that elementary school was coming to an end, I was quickly realizing that I was expected to start preparing for middle school without time to catch my breath. I realized I would be starting the advocacy for middle school while Marissa was still in elementary school.

I did not feel like the personnel were ready to hear about the curriculum supports and modifications that had enabled us to support Marissa. It was possible they were worried they would not meet be able to meet her needs. We felt like we were leaving the warm familiarity of elementary school. It was time to start building new relationships.

As I stood outside the elementary school waiting for Marissa, it became clear to me that I was not feeling like I was continuing Marissa's education in school. I felt like I was starting completely over.

The first marking period of fifth grade was already finished. I was full of worry. How could all of the training about her accommodations and equipment that we had established since kindergarten be transferred to middle school before the end of the school year? I felt afraid our work would be lost in the transition.

The bell rang. I greeted Marissa with a smile and told her how happy I was to see her. Then I picked up my son along with some neighborhood children. They patiently waited for me as I honored my carpool commitment.

As usual, my son had a matter-of-fact recollection of his school day. He told me that for the past few days he had been eating lunch with Marissa. I told him that I thought that was kind of him. He looked a little puzzled and replied, "No, Mom, I just like being with her." However, he explained that he didn't think that the paraprofessional that helped Marissa remembered who he was. I made a mental note to tell the paraprofessional that the boy who had been sitting by her at lunch was her brother.

We went to pick up my youngest son at preschool. I'm always greeted with a running hug from him and "Mommy!" The greeting always makes me feel like this has been the most important thing that has happened for him all day.

Arriving home at the end of the day with all of my children is one of my favorite times. I always have a moment of gratefulness that we are all together again. This feeling soon fades as I rush to get dinner for everyone.

While making dinner, I spoke with our advocate on the telephone. In order to be helpful to us and Marissa, it was important that I take the time to keep her up to date. My husband had returned home to work in his home office. Since he attended the meeting at school in the afternoon, he would be working late.

After dinner, as usual, we followed our daily routine of homework, baths, and bedtime. When the children were asleep, I called my friend that is a high school principal. We talked for an hour, and

I went to bed feeling a little better about my middle school encounter. Sometimes it is helpful to get another person's perspective.

Wednesday: Brief relief, then more worry

I went to work as I always do. I work part-time every morning until noon. I came home from work determined to tackle the household chores that seemed to be getting away from me. However, some of my chores were finished, while the rest were left undone because Marissa had Girl Scouts after school. I always needed to assist her in the meetings. My husband took over my carpool responsibilities and picked up our youngest son.

We came home from Girl Scouts at five o'clock. We started the after school routine of dinner, homework, and bedtime.

I explained to Paul my excitement of seeing Marissa's progress at Girl Scouts. While we waited for the meeting to begin, Marissa independently drew a circle after I asked her to do it. The coordination to do this is difficult for her. My feeling of worry from the previous day's meeting had faded. It was replaced with the love and hope I saw in my daughter.

After the children were in bed and the backpacks were packed, I managed to reassemble the inside of the house again. As the middle school personnel requested, I composed an email to the director of special education requesting a meeting. However, I was interrupted. My husband called for me to come upstairs. Marissa was having a mild seizure.

Did this mean we needed to adjust her daily medication? After giving Marissa medication to stop the seizure, I called and left a message for the nurse at the neurologist's office. I knew it was midnight, but this gave her time the next day to return my call. I also finished my email to the special education director.

Thursday: Added worry turns into stress

I had agreed to attend an all-day seminar on the education of children with autism. In order to allow everyone on Marissa's IEP team to attend, we agreed to keep Marissa home from school. My husband agreed to stay with her. He spent the day trying to meet her needs and to work from home as needed.

We often do not talk about the demands of having a child with special needs at work. When we have meetings for school and doctor's appointments, we must move our schedules around to be available for our family. This creates a lot of stress as we try to fulfill the role of being parents of a child with special needs and work.

> Do not feel guilty about the time you spend attending to your child's needs.

Luckily, families with children with special needs have developed great skills in multi-tasking. Do not feel guilty about the time you spend attending to your child's needs. Chances are you are a dedicated employee with a clear focus on being successful at work since you feel the importance of providing for your child. In addition, you have a wonderful sense of compassion for others that has been developed simply by having a child with special needs.

While Paul was with Marissa, I went to the seminar with Marissa's current IEP team. I wanted them to feel appreciated. However, I wanted to give honest input about how it feels to be the parent of a child with special needs. I felt the stress of wanting to do and say the right things all day at the meeting on Marissa's behalf.

After I returned home from the conference, Marissa's neurologist returned my call. Indeed we needed to adjust her medication.

Friday: Basketball snacks, are you kidding?

Early in the morning while I was making lunches for school, I took a moment to send an email to Marissa's teacher. Since being on medication is related to Marissa's disability, we asked for accommodations in her IEP to adjust her work in the school day as needed. Instead of being asked to perform many tasks independently, she would instead be shown the task or work on easier tasks. School personnel asked that I send an email to them when medication changed and accommodations were needed. I explained that her medication had been adjusted, she may appear sleepy, and could they please make adjustments as needed. I briefly thought about calling to follow up with my email, but decided the email was enough.

After school, Marissa looked sad and tired. The paraprofessionals asked me if the medication had been changed. It was quickly clear to me that my email message was not clear enough. Therefore, Marissa was sad from a difficult day at school. I felt guilty that I had not called school to double-check that Marissa's needs would be met.

My neighbor called to see if I was going to my friend's home party at six o'clock. I figured out the email went to my husband and I had not known about the invitation. I called my friend to explain that I could not attend. She was nice, but hoped I could just "stop by."

My son had a basketball game that was also at six o'clock, two hours earlier than I anticipated. At five o'clock, I had figured out that it was my night to bring the snack for the team.

This was a week that felt almost impossible to get through. Was the week almost over? I didn't think I could handle one more thing. I managed to get my son to his basketball game with the snacks. I allowed myself to feel okay about not attending my friend's home party.

Later that night, Marissa woke up with another seizure. It was possible the medication was not yet regulated. My husband was dismayed when I gave Marissa the medication she needed and I returned to bed, leaving

I have learned that eventually the storm settles, followed by an appreciated calm.

him in charge of Marissa. It is an unwritten law that we both stay up with her since a prolonged seizure will result in a call to EMS. It seems that whenever I am sure I will not be able to handle one more thing, I seem to always get one more thing.

In the beginning, the highs and lows of having a child with special needs seemed unmanageable to me. There were many doctor's appointments, therapy sessions, and meetings to attend. However, I have learned there are many uneventful weeks.

While the week I had just experienced seemed almost impossible to manage both emotionally and physically, I have learned that eventually the storm settles, followed by an appreciated calm. I use the calm weeks to reorganize my family and prepare for the busy days I know will often unexpectedly happen.

Important Points to Remember

- I am supposed to be a model of an adult living a well-adjusted, happy life.

- I know I will best support my child with special needs in an environment of order.

- Try not to schedule two meetings at school in one week.

- Do not expect that people will be ready to fully hear your message the first time you meet. You have probably taken several years to formulate your thoughts— give people a few meetings to consider your ideas for themselves. Whether you like it or not, this may be new to them.

- As a parent of a child with special needs, you will have some weeks that seem almost impossible to manage. Use the calm weeks to prepare for the busy weeks you know will come.

Chapter 13
Home Skills

When I was first learning how to manage a family, I attended Christian conferences for stay-at-home moms. There were women that figured out how to keep their houses clean throughout the week. There were women that have figured out how to grocery shop for a month at a time. There were women that were skilled in developing their children's religious faith. I listened to them, and I learned how to develop my skills as a mother.

At these conferences, I was also reminded that I was not the only person raising our children. My husband and I needed to maintain our roles as the center of our family. I needed to honor his role as my children's father. If he took the time to get them dressed, then I would not comment if their clothes did not match.

My husband helps the children with their homework. Often he does not explain the math problem to Marissa until after she watches him do it. I always talk her through it. I have realized that my way is not the only way to do things around our house.

> Sharing the responsibility of caring for our family with my husband allows us to support one another.

Since we have a child with special needs, my husband did not have the option of becoming a hands-off dad. Marissa required our assistance. I needed to become less interested in being perfect and develop my skills as a mother of three children.

Sharing the responsibility of caring for our family with my husband allows us to support one another. We become a team that depends on one another for success. This year my three-year-old son started preschool. On the questionnaire from school I was asked, "Are there any unusual circumstances at home we should know about?"

I wrote, "Andrew's older sister has autism. Therefore, our family is very close." Having a child in the family with a disability creates an opportunity to build closeness.

There is no shame in having a child or a sibling with a disability. Marissa is her own person. The responsibility for her behaviors should not be felt by her siblings or by her parents. We guide her and work as a family to help her develop into an independent adult. In our family, we help one another. Fairness means that everyone gets what they need—not just everyone getting the same. In addition, the responsibility for Marissa's successes does not belong to her siblings or to her parents. They belong to Marissa. We celebrate her successes with her, as well as the successes of our other children with each of them.

> Fairness means that everyone gets what they need—not just everyone getting the same.

My husband and I have many things to discuss. We discuss school. We also discuss doctors, therapies, bills, and of course, the other two children. It is also important to talk about us. Since we are the center of the family, we cannot get lost in the list of things to discuss.

> Make the effort to stay connected to your spouse.

Make the effort to stay connected to your spouse. I notice that he is pretty good with text messaging, so my phone has a keyboard. Since he attends many meetings and appointments, we talk on the way in and out.

Someone told me, "Men will talk more while participating in an activity outside of the home." So I stopped trying to talk to him when he's watching television. He's most relaxed and open to discussions when we go out.

Hiring a babysitter allows me to reconnect with my spouse. We tried not talking about "serious" things while we were out, but for us we often need that time to talk about what happened that week.

It is important that your children see you make your spouse a priority. Children like to know someone is in charge at their house. They need their parents at the center of their family. Do not let your child with special needs become the center of your home—she has parents for

> Do not let your child with special needs become the center of your home.

that. If you are feeling stressed in your marriage and cannot get along, get counseling.

At many conferences I attend, the experts say, "85 percent of families with children with special needs have parents that are divorced." It takes my breath away every time I hear this. Of course the stress of medical worries and bills weighs on a marriage. However, I have seen many mothers that shut out their spouses and take over their children with special needs. It is important to try to work as a team at home.

The days we feel unwelcome at our neighborhood school and in our community add stress to our marriage. However, we share the common goal of creating a loving family.

My husband and I are making a life in the community for our family. This includes our daughter attending our neighborhood school. I think our focus on our family cements us together. Pulling a child away from their neighborhood peers and community to go to a separate school adds another element of stress on the family. In addition, I think the feeling that "someone else" will care for this child seems like it makes it easier for dads to walk away when children are put in a school for children with special needs.

School personnel should not make you feel like they are taking over your responsibilities. You and your husband are your child's primary caregivers. They should be assisting you in your life-journey of raising your child.

Since returning to work, I have been paying close attention to the families that have their children with special needs fully included in their neighborhood schools. I have not yet met a family that has experienced divorce.

Take time to take care of yourself.

Take the time to take care of yourself. It will make you feel better. I have the same routine every morning. I take a shower, fix my hair, and put on makeup. I usually do this on the weekends and holidays too. While I was pregnant, a mother told me, "Just wait, you won't have time for showers anymore."

I tried it out a few times. I took Marissa to school in my sweatpants without a shower. It never failed; this would be the day the director asked to speak with me. Or Marissa would be sick and this was the day I would show up at the doctor's office feeling unprepared. Taking a shower makes me feel ready for the day. I feel more confident and professional. I feel more alert. If my shirt gets dirty, I change it. It is important that I take time to take care of myself.

I go through cycles of exercising. Overall, I am a better parent when I feel fit. If Marissa has been up a lot at night, I skip my favorite television show to go to bed early. I try to feed my children healthy foods so they will be well. I try to eat well so I also will feel healthy.

The more self-respect I have, the more others will respect me. This means I can ultimately be a better wife, mother, friend, and professional.

It is a tough job being a mother. It is a tougher job, and sometimes almost an impossible job, being a parent of a child with special needs. However, if you are going somewhere important—which is probably almost daily—you will need to figure out a self-care routine that works for you. If you are going to an IEP meeting with teachers, dress nicely and fix your hair.

You also need to find a routine for making sure your child is bathed and dressed in clean clothes daily. Their hair must be kept. I remember going to a training meeting with other parents of children with special needs. The dad of a child with Down's syndrome explained, "People are already judging my child harshly. Dressing him well gives him an advantage he can use."

Marissa likes playing in the dirt. She will pick it up and let it fall to the ground. She even likes letting it fall over her head and then onto the ground. You can imagine how dirty she gets playing. My job is to help her maintain her self-respect in a community that may not understand why she is doing this. It is also important for me to help her develop social skills. So I may redirect her to drop the dirt into a bucket. Ultimately I think it is healthy for kids to get dirty and to let them play. However, when she is done, I help her wipe her hands and face so she is presentable.

One year, Marissa had a paraprofessional that let her get dirty while she was playing during recess. When I picked Marissa up from school, her face and hands were still dirty. I was relieved she had a great time at recess. But since Marissa needs additional assistance, people notice her as they walk by at school. I explained this to the paraprofessional and asked her to make sure Marissa's hands and face were clean after coming inside from recess. Socially, people are less likely to interact with you if you are dirty.

I heard a mother explain that they could not afford to dress their child in the latest fashions. Do not take advantage of your child's disability. If they could tell you what they wanted to wear, what would they say? Visiting resale shops may be helpful. I know of a teacher that asked parents in the class for donations. You do not want schools to only focus on your child's disabilities. You must also consider the typical problems many mothers face in having their children look presentable at school.

As a teacher, I occasionally had a student in class that did not bathe regularly. This is problematic. We are teaching children to value others. Yet socially, it is difficult to work with someone that does not smell clean. You must make sure your child is clean. If this is difficult, you may need to hire behavioral supports at home to help you through this issue.

I have met mothers that are very happy staying at home without an outside job. I have also met mothers that seem to feel like martyrs. Some stay at home, yet they criticize others for working. I think mothers must do what makes them happy. In my case, I was trained to teach. It allows me to contribute to the community. It helps me stay current on the educational research so I can help support my children at school. It also prevents me from becoming overly involved in Marissa's daily education. I want her teachers to feel capable of meeting her needs. I want Marissa to know she can be independent without me.

At a meeting with our financial planner, he explained that my income was putting us into the next tax bracket. Financially, it did not make much sense for me to work. However, in the teaching profession we are paid by seniority. If I quit my job and

> Take the time to make a quality life for you and your family. Work smarter, not harder, to manage your life well and to build your happiness.

returned later, I would lose my seniority. I would lose my placement in a building with teachers that I enjoyed working with. Also, my skills would become outdated. Working part-time was a good solution for me.

I think it is important for all mothers to feel fulfilled and happy. I heard a financial planner explain that women give away too much of their time for free. I think it is important to work toward good causes. However, there is nothing wrong with getting paid.

> Having quiet time with my family is a luxury that only I can claim for them.

Your child will probably have homework. You may be asked to fill in questionnaires and return them to school. It is very important that you thoughtfully and completely support your child in completing this work. It will give your child background knowledge about what the class is doing. It will also let the teacher know that you value their work with your child. Complete the work. Turn it in on time or early.

Carefully use your time. My husband says, "Save Marissa first. Save the world second." Sometimes I pass up invitations simply because we had a busy week. Having quiet time with my family is a luxury that only I can claim for them.

In the past, I often volunteered to make dinners and visit relatives more frequently. I think it is important to maintain my role as a mother, sister, daughter, friend, etc. It occurred to me that if they understood what was happening in my life, they may understand that sometimes I need to rest.

Helping your child with special needs is an important, time-consuming job. However, this is not your only responsibility. We must live the kind of lives we hope our children to have. I think many families are running through life. Your child with special needs will make you slow down. Take the time to make a quality life for you and your family. Work smarter, not harder, to manage your life well and to build your happiness.

Important Points to Remember

- My husband and I need to maintain our roles as the center of our family.

- Work with your spouse to share the day-to-day responsibilities that come with having children.

- If you are the only adult in your household, find others to help support you and your family.

- There is no shame in having a child or a sibling with a disability.

- Fairness means that everyone gets what they need—not just everyone getting the same.

- Take the time to take care of yourself.

- The day you wear fuzzy slippers in the car to drop off your children will be the day the principal needs to speak with you.

- Every day you need to make sure your child is bathed, your child's teeth and hair are brushed, and they are dressed in age-appropriate clothing.

- Make sure school personnel can easily reach you during the day as needed.

- Take time to create quiet time with your family. It is a luxury only you can create for them.

Chapter 14
Review

You may want to review the following list yearly to help you remain focused on your goal of including your child in their neighborhood school.

- Understand that your primary job is to be your child's advocate. It is important to stay focused on your goal—to have your child included in school.

- Hold your head up high and smile at the people you meet when you are with your child. This means that even if your child is refusing to keep their shoes or clothing on, you will act like this is no big deal. It is in the best interest of your child for you to remain rational, but you must also understand that other people (parents, teachers, principals) are watching you. You are showing others how you expect your child to be treated. Often children with special needs cannot express their need to be treated with dignity, so you need to always be your child's advocate and model appropriate interaction.

- Be proud of your child. Your child's needs are nothing to be embarrassed or ashamed about. I believe your child belongs in school just like everyone else.

- My ninety-five-year-old aunt reminds me that this is an honorable job. Great moments are the times we get a genuine smile or an offer of true assistance from another person.

- Always be gracious. Never be mean. The inclusion of children with special needs into the classroom is not a "typical" public school practice. Your job is to educate the people you meet about why this is important.

- Do not "over-educate" people about why your child is in school. You want your child to have typical school experiences. You need to talk about the typical interests your child has.

- Your child must come to school neat and clean-looking. You are already facing many obstacles. In our society, people place value on how people look. This is much of the prejudice facing a person with special needs. Of course our daughter loves to play in the dirt at recess, but her hands and face must be clean after play.

- You must be kind and polite to everyone. Be professional. The people you are interacting with are working with your child every day. While I believe it is your child's right to be there, you are asking people to do things they are not used to doing.

- When you are in meetings for your child, always have their list of IEP goals (the yearly goals) with you. Anything you request for your child should be tied to these goals.

- You must take an advocate with you to all meetings. The advocate you bring should not be there to "get you what you want" but to assist you in clearly communicating your needs. They must know what the law allows, and they must know *before the meeting* what areas you are willing to compromise in. Remember to notify those involved that an advocate will be attending the meeting. Smile. You do not want people to feel threatened. Having an advocate helps everyone remain honest about what was said (ask your advocate to take notes for you).

- Call your advocate prior to a meeting. Discuss the goal of the meeting. Discuss the outcome you want them to help you to achieve. Tell your advocate that their primary job is to listen. Sometimes our advocate only speaks once or not at all during a meeting, but having her by our side completely changes the tone of the meeting.

- Try to have your husband accompany you to all the meetings. (If you are not married, then some other consistent man must accompany you—maybe a grandpa?) My husband and I agree to back each other up at our meetings and to be a united front. There is nothing more impressive than a family working to support their child. If we are angry before the meeting or we disagree, we have agreed to discuss this outside of the meeting.

- Demand (in a professional, smiling way) that your child be treated using the least dangerous assumption. This means that everyone working with your child will assume they are intelligent and understand the concepts being explained in the general education curriculum. You want your child to have access to general education with modifications to the daily assignments that will allow your child to participate along with the class.

- Get outside professional assistance for your child. Do not expect the public school to "take over" your child's education. You have the responsibility to continually seek outside therapy as needed for your child. This will help give direction to what is being done in school. Remember that school may not be the place for the best "therapy"—school is the place for learning the lessons of life and receiving an education among peers.

- Remember the goal of your child in public school: to be included in the life-experience of attending their neighborhood school and to have access to the general educational curriculum.

- Take good care of yourself and your family. Develop the skills needed to run an organized, productive, and healthy home.

Resources

As a parent of a child with special needs, you will be researching the best practices of education for your child. Here is a list of helpful resources to help you begin your work.

Books

Zemelman, Steven, Harvey Daniels, and Arthur Hyde. *Best Practice: New Standards for Teaching and Learning in America's Schools*. Portsmouth, NH: Heinemann, 1998.

This book gives you basic information about what teachers have learned about good instruction. If I did not have a degree in teaching, I would start by reading this book as a foundation for understanding what teachers already know.

Websites

The Arc
www.thearc.org

"The Arc of the United States advocates for the rights and full participation of all children and adults with intellectual and developmental disabilities. Together with our network of members and affiliated chapters, we improve systems of supports and services; connect families; inspire communities; and influence public policy."

Lekotek
www.lekotek.org

"Lekotek uses interactive play experiences, and the learning that results, to promote the inclusion of children with special needs into family and community life."

Autism Society of America
www.autism-society.org

"ASA, the nation's leading grassroots autism organization, exists to improve the lives of all affected by autism. We do this by increasing public awareness about the day-to-day issues faced by people on the spectrum, advocating for appropriate services for individuals across the lifespan, and providing the latest information regarding treatment, education, research, and advocacy."

Autism Research Institute
www.autism.com

"The Autism Research Institute (ARI), a non-profit organization, was established in 1967. For more than forty years, ARI has devoted its work to conducting research, and to disseminating the results of research, on the triggers of autism and on methods of diagnosing and treating autism. We provide research-based information to parents and professionals around the world."

Autism Research Institute/DAN
www.autism.com/dan/danusdis.htm

This section of the website contains a list of doctors associated with DAN (Defeat Autism Now).

TASH
www.tash.org

"TASH is an international membership association leading the way to inclusive communities through research, education, and advocacy."

University of Northern Iowa
www.uni.edu/coe/inclusion/philosophy

This section of UNI's website explains the philosophy of inclusive education and the benefits of the inclusive classroom for all students.

Dance of Partnership
www.danceofpartnership.com

"Janice Fialka, MSW, ACSW, is a national trainer, presenter, and advocate on issues related to disability. She is the author of three books, numerous articles, poems, and the newly produced CD of three of her poems accompanied by original piano music and stunning visuals."

Grand Valley State University START Program
www.gvsu.edu/autismcenter/

"The Statewide Autism Resources and Training (START) project is a state-funded project designed to provide training and technical assistance to educators in Michigan that serve students with Autism Spectrum Disorders (ASD). The START project has been in place for seven years through the support of the Michigan Department of Education, Office of Special Education, and Early Intervention Services."

ERIC (Educational Resource Information Center)
www.eric.ed.gov.ERICDocs/Data/ericdocs2sql/content_ storage_01/0000019b/80/14/15/2c.pdf

This link takes you to a research article that describes the benefits of inclusion.

Michigan Department of Education
www.ccsso.org/content/PDFs/Bauer.ppt

This link takes you to a PowerPoint presentation that was presented in March 2006 about universal education.

RTI (Response To Intervention) Action Network
www.rtinetwork.org/Learn/Diversity/ar/ DisproportionateRepresentation

This section of the RTI Action Network website discusses response to intervention and the disproportionate representation of culturally and linguistically diverse students in special education.

United States Department of Education
www.ed.gov

This is the United States Department of Education's website and includes national curriculum objectives, laws, and other valuable educational resources.

Michigan Department of Education
www.michigan.gov/mde

This is the State of Michigan's Department of Education's website and includes information such as state curriculum objectives, laws, and other valuable educational resources. You are encouraged to Google your own state's educational website.

Hearts at Home
www.hearts-at-home.org

This website contains helpful information for mothers.

About.com: Feng Shui
fengshui.about.com/ home organization

"Feng Shui is an ancient art and science developed over three thousand years ago in China. It is a complex body of knowledge that reveals how to balance the energies of any given space to assure the health and good fortune for people inhabiting it."

The Clean Team
www.thecleanteam.com

This website contains helpful information for speed cleaning, clutter control, and overall maintenance of your home.

HGTV
www.hgtv.com

This website contains useful information about home organization.

Suze Orman
www.suzeorman.com

This website contains useful information about finances.

Author Biography

Jennifer Greening, Ed.S., lives, works, and plays with her husband and three children in Southeastern Michigan. While teaching, she has earned many degrees in the field of education. She believes her greatest education has occurred while holding the hand of her child with disabilities. She enthusiastically shares her vision of all children learning together in their neighborhood schools. Please visit her website at www.jennifergreeningbooks.com.